We've Always Been Free

We've Always Been Free

Poems, Reveries, Short Stories, photos and other musings of growing up in Chagrin Falls Park, Ohio

ANDERSON HITCHCOCK

iUniverse, Inc.
Bloomington

We've Always Been Free
Poems, Reveries, Short Stories, photos and other musings of growing up in
Chagrin Falls Park, Ohio

iUniverse books may be ordered through booksellers or by contacting:

iUniverse
1663 Liberty Drive
Bloomington, IN 47403
www.iuniverse.com
1-800-Authors (1-800-288-4677)

Because of the dynamic nature of the Internet, any web addresses or links contained in this book may have changed since publication and may no longer be valid. The views expressed in this work are solely those of the author and do not necessarily reflect the views of the publisher, and the publisher hereby disclaims any responsibility for them.

Any people depicted in stock imagery provided by Thinkstock are models, and such images are being used for illustrative purposes only.
Certain stock imagery © Thinkstock.

ISBN: 978-1-4759-6566-7 (sc)
ISBN: 978-1-4759-6567-4 (ebk)

Printed in the United States of America

iUniverse rev. date: 12/06/2012

CONTENTS

Photo Descriptions..vii

Foreword...5

In Memoriam To..9

Home Room..15

Have You Heard the Sidewalk Cricket Sing............................28

Small Town America...32

Lay Lightly on the Concrete..35

Sea of Reality..36

Koi...37

Unrequited Lovers..38

Sirens in the Night...41

The Harlem to Leimert Park Convention.............................43

The Brown Paper Bag..46

P.O.W..49

The Indomitable Black Man...51

Affiliate of the Ghetto..61

I've reached My Limit Baby..68

We've Always Been Free...71

Run Nigger Run...74

The Cornfield..77

Zakiyah's Poen (Oh Diaspora)...80

Niggeritis...85

The Master Physician...91

Why Willow Trees Weep..96

The Hourglass Poet..101

Raise a Toast..136

When God Met Juan..138

Valerie's Poem..143

A Kwanzaa Poem...146

The Wind Chime Tree...149

About the Author...155

Tell It Like It Tis, Not Like It Twas (JT's Poem)...............160

Author's Statement...167

Author's History..169

Photo Descriptions

Pg. 108 Cousin Tyrone and Son; Valley Lounge Saloon;

Pg. 109 Celebration of African History Month.

Pg. 110 Valley Lounge

Pg. 111 Local Negro League Baseball Team.

Pg. 112 Church gathering (Zion Hill Missionary Baptist Church) 1950's

Pg. 113 Lula and Felton Hitchcock (mid 1950's)

Pg. 114-115 Community Center Staff (Lula Hitchcock, Rose Motley, Martha Brown, Ms. Ward and Jim Jackson; Community Volunteer Fire Fighters; Road conditions highlighted in news article.

Pg. 116-117 Hitchcock Family, Felton, Lula, Felton Jr., George, Anderson and Milton; Lula and Felton Hitchcock; music lesson for youth.

Pg. 117-119 Huff's Tavern; Cousin Tyrone on American Flag; Congregation at Zion Hill Missionary Baptist Church.

Pg. 119-120 Court House demonstration follows the murder of a local resident by Geauga County Sheriff's Deputies; residents playing volleyball; Center secretary Martha Brown.

Pg. 121-122 Author kneeling at the fall; a Zion Hill Missionary Baptist Church woman's gathering.

Pg. 122-123 Gathering of young women and young mothers; Cover of Book "A place of their own" written by Andrew Weiss; Chagrin Falls All Stars.

Pg. 124 Author before graduating from Kenston High School in 1965. Black students graduated last in a class of 94 students; Prom party (Larry Long, Kathryn Taylor, Nara Chillous, Nathaniel Greene); Felton Hitchcock and his date; Aunt Virginia and Husband Bob Anderson

Pg. 125 Author dressed for prom with younger brother Bill; San Jose Family (Alice and Desiree Covarrubias, Cousin Larry Long, Mother Lula Hitchcock, Brother George, Clarence Harris (wine), and cat (Maya).

Pg. 126 Anderson with brothers George, Felton and Milton (1954); Grandparents Genie and Luke Walker with Uncle Will and Ms. Huff on their way to Church; Grandmother at the side of her house.

Pg. 127 Artie Brooks interviews local resident; Cleveland Foundation Grant to assist the community.

Pg. 128 Author graduates from first grade at Park Elementary School (1954) Anderson is seated bottom row extreme left.

Pg. 129 Reverend and Mrs. Riggins seated in front of congregation of Zion Hill Missionary Baptist Church (1940's)

Pg. 130 Author playing bongos with friend, while in Army stationed at Fairbanks, Alaska (1969); community photo

Pg. 131 Community Gathering

Pg. 131 Mrs. Adams; J. C. Head.

Pg. 132-133 Chagrin Falls Park Fire Department

Pg. 134 Huff's Bar

Pg. 135 Chagrin Valley All Stars

From left to right: Mr. Rodgers; Mr. Elijah Norman; Mr. Felton (Hunny) Hitchcock; Mr. Charles (Shug) Walker; Mr. Paris; Mr. Wheeler; Mr. Bloxsom; Mr. Hardy; Mr. Calvin Long; Mr. Huff; Mr. E.J. Lynch

(This photograph now hangs in the Black Firefighters Hall of Fame in Los Angeles, California)

WE'VE ALWAYS BEEN FREE

Poems, Reveries, Short Stories, photos and other musings of growing up in Chagrin Falls Park, Ohio

By Anderson Hitchcock

Featuring "Have you heard the sidewalk cricket sing", "The Wind Chime Tree" and "The Harlem to Leimert Park Convention

Anderson is also the Author of three other books, "Economics as a Second Language", Creating Wealth One Family Reunion at a Time; OtherHolics Anonymous; and Health, Wealth and Prosperity

THOSE WHO CAN'T DO

TEACH

THOSE WHO CAN'T TEACH

WRITE

THOSE WHO CAN'T WRITE

LABOR

THOSE WHO CAN'T LABOR

PILLAGE, PLUNDER AND STEAL

THOSE WHO CAN'T PILLAGE, PLUNDER AND STEAL

PREACH

"He who chooses his own master, is no longer a slave" Plato

Foreword

The bitter sweet survival of freed black men and women is perfectly captured by Anderson, as he sets the pain of denial to the lyrics of poetry. We've Always Been Free retells a story from across this nation, a story of strength and determination in the face of an ever moving promise of freedom. This story can be retold about towns and villages from Florida, Oklahoma, Kansas, North and South Dakota, Iowa, California and wherever those freed from slavery sought to carve out their dreams in a never ending fight against racism. The Chagrin Falls Park, Ohio stand symbolizes all the struggles of our people, as freedom continues to be grasped with one hand while being yanked away by another hand.

Anderson's story is a memorial to his life and his ancestors in Chagrin Falls Park, Ohio, told in a setting of poetry that captures the sweet sounds and warm feelings of those shielding and protecting loved ones from the bitter reality of life worn thin by lack and deprivation. What an ideal time for such a critical recounting of a past that continues to live as the leader of the world's most powerful advocate for freedom, experience the harsh repudiation of racism.

Get ready, as "We've Always Been Free" takes you on a roller coaster ride of emotions, from the fright of a thirteen year old boy jailed unjustly, to his release to the cheers and love of his community. This is a ride from yesterday as newly freed slaves of yesterday experience today as newly economically enslaved. Anderson's use of photography, prose and poetry colors the ride while sourcing all your emotions.

Thank you, Anderson, for the journey to the Wind Chime Tree.

Dr. Wilma L. Kirchhofer, MPH, PHD

"Give a man a fish, he can feed his family for a day; teach a man to fish, he can feed his family for a life time, but he must have access to the lake; Only! <u>Ownership guarantees access</u>"

Anderson Hitchcock

I would like to thank Kenya Cher Bey Esq., for editing this book and, Both she and Shilo Bey for allowing me the space in their home in Philadelphia to write. I would also like to thank Ms. Angela Darling and Family in the Bronx for their kindness during the writing of this book and lastly I want to thank Mori and Ghenea for giving me the impetus to leave this legacy.

In Memoriam To

This book of poetry, reveries, short stories, photos and musings is dedicated to the pioneers of Chagrin Falls Park, Ohio. This, approximately 110 square acre, area was settled in the early twentieth century by a group of African Americans, who were looking for their American Dream. My Grandparents, Genie and Luke Walker moved to Chagrin Falls Park in a fortuitous move, just months before the stock market crash of 1929.

Chagrin Falls Park became, among other things, a symbol of Independence, hard work and perseverance, which thrived for nearly eight decades before the County of Geauga, in collusion with the township of Bainbridge, decided for political expediency and unmitigated political chutzpa to destroy the historic nature of this traditional Black Community. With malice a forth thought, and with considerable Gaul and underhandedness, these political conspirators took control of the very soul of the community, the Chagrin Falls Park Community Center. It is a saga of moral and political decadence, which needs to be told.

While it might be too late for this wrong to be redressed and the community to be saved for the current residents and for posterity, it is a story which needs to be examined for its relevance to the future of similar communities that may still exist somewhere in America.

Chagrin Falls is a town adjacent to its namesake, which fits the term bucolic to a tee and is located in an area of Ohio that is unmatched in its beauty and Americana. In the 1980s a movie, which dealt with a traditional Thanksgiving Day in America, the producers chose this town to represent a New England Town. Due to political gerrymandering and the desire to separate these two communities along racial and economic lines Chagrin Falls and Chagrin Falls Park, found themselves in separate counties and with separate governing bodies, although the economies of both areas were and still remain to this day inextricably linked. So began the saga of the decimation of a culture and a people's way of life.

Further, as if separating these two communities, into two different counties was not sufficient to accomplish their nefarious goal of decimating their culture and way of life, the school district authorities directed that the children of Chagrin Falls Park be bused past Chagrin Falls schools, to those located eight miles away from home. Because of the way that the school district lines had been drawn, the children who, in many cases, were within walking distance of these schools, could not attend them, but instead were bused to either Bainbridge Middle School or Kenston High School. This situation remains the same today.

In the near eight decades since the redistricting was imposed, it is estimated that millions of dollars in sales taxes paid by residents of Chagrin Falls Park on items purchased in Chagrin Falls shopping area went into the coiffures of a city which denied Chagrin Falls Park shoppers their inherent and basic civil and social rights.

In the Chagrin Falls Library, where I spent a lot of time as a young man, one can read stories of colonialist 200 years ago killing native Americans fore sport. As these stories recount, the early residents wonder how the families of these Native Americans would feel, when they realize that their fathers, husbands or sons would not be coming home that day or ever. This is the same attitude that was pervasive during my formative years, but this story is not about me, it is about an area, a community, a way of life which recently came to an end, because of a lack of historical prescience and blind sightedness about the future of gallant people, the residents of Chagrin Falls Park.

In the 1970s and 80s this quiet little town became a tourist destination, primarily for Clevelanders seeking to get out into the country and this weekend exodus became the death knell for the lifestyle which most people who lived here valued. I remember swimming in the falls as a child before the throngs of tourist found the town to be inviting for day long excursions out of the city.

There was then a prohibition against swimming sign posted near our favorite swimming hole right under the bridge. This pretty much eliminated swimming in this location from that point onward.

There are a few individuals of note who at some point called Chagrin Falls, Ohio home and they are Tim Conway, actor, who lived on Bell Street, a few houses down from Bell Telephone Company and Hart Crane, poet who lived on a second floor walk up in the heart of Chagrin Falls, which had a picturesque view. He committed suicide there. Arguably the most famous resident of Chagrin Falls Park would have to be Cynthia King, who grew up in the Park and went on to become, long before Tyra Bank, the first black super model with her billboards for Virginia Slim. Other than these few, residents of this area remained pretty much out of the spotlight.

This area of Ohio very much however remains in the hearts of those who have ever called it home. In a way, these two disparate communities epitomize the divisions, which have allowed racial antagonism to remain so very ingrained in the American Culture, and throughout Americas' cultural history to become pervasive.

I would be remiss if not to express my love for this place and sincere appreciation for having grown up in it, in spite of all of the pernicious aspects of racism, which made this northern small town seem, more like a rural Mississippi town, complete with shotgun houses, burning crosses and rules of social engagement that dictated how people related one to another. I remember sitting in a restaurant, waiting for over an hour to order breakfast with my late Aunt Ella Long, before leaving just as hungry as when we had come in. I also remember walking into a restaurant in Chagrin Falls and hearing a young child say, " . . . ooh mommy, look at the nigger". Or in preparation to purchase either shoes or hats, it was necessary to take a piece of string that was used to determine my shoe or hat size, because we were not allowed to try these items on in the store prior to purchasing them.

Chagrin Falls Park, however, very much remains in the hearts of those people who have ever called this place home. In a way, these two disparate communities highlight the divisions, which have allowed racial antagonism to remain so very ingrained in the American Culture, and throughout its History to become pervasive.

Having set this scene, it is incumbent upon me to express my sincere love and appreciation for having grown up in this area. In spite of all of the pernicious aspects of racism, which made this northern small town seem, more like a rural Mississippi town, complete with shotgun houses, burning crosses and rules of social engagement that dictated how people related one to another?

I only relate these stories in order to set the ambiance for the poems and reveries contained in this book and to highlight the unfairness that has caused the residents still living in Chagrin Falls Park to lose control of their community.

While growing up In Chagrin Falls Park, we limited our contact with Chagrin Falls and relied upon the support and ingenuity of the residents of Chagrin Falls Park. The residents of Chagrin Falls Park, were some of the most talented, Kind, and caring community conscious people, in the world.

Park residents depended upon their own resiliency, combined with their own God given talents for their livelihoods, liberties and for whatever pursuits of happiness they could find.

The Park was a small but self-contained community. It had its own stores, gas stations, bars, Churches, community center, social clubs, youth programs and all that was required to live somewhat healthy and happy lives. One photo in this book shows the Chagrin Falls Park Volunteer Fire Department (Page 111), which came about after much loss of life, due to the continually slow response of the township fire department, which would often take up to an hour to response to a call of fire in the Park. This photo highlights the independence of the residents of Chagrin Falls Park.

I was educated for the first seven grades, in a one-room schoolhouse, in the middle of the community, which was built by the community in order to educate the children of the community. In this school, all seven grades met in one room and studied everything from mathematics to science and social studies without any contact with the outside world. We were totally self-contained, and the school, as well as the community, acted as an incubator for the intellectual and self-reliant fulfillment that many African Americans sought during those years, and most continue to seek today.

The usage of the Yiddish word "Chutzpah" accurately reflects how the Park community came to be. A few years before the great stock market crash of 1929 a Jewish newspaper editor had purchased this property, ostensibly to build a summer retreat for Jews living in and around Cleveland. However, prior to the construction of the first home in this area, a group of the residents of Chagrin Falls found out about the scheme and true to form, decided to burn a cross on the property.

The incident caused great consternation in the Jewish community and forced the owner to abandon his scheme. The editor, also being the publisher of the Negro Digest, decided that rather than to lose his investment, he would sub divide the property into five feet by twenty-five feet lots and sell them. So without divulging the racial animus, he ran an ad in the Negro Digest offering to sell lots, for five dollars per lot.

Others purchased property at Sheriffs sale, unsuspecting the cold shoulder that awaited them from the all white town of Chagrin Falls proper. I would wager this is a pattern of neglect that persisted throughout much of the country, were the aspirations of a significant part of the population were exposed to the Pollyanna vision of the so-called "majority" population.

Needless to say, in ignorance, the land was quickly purchased principally by Cleveland's black population, creating an exodus of those seeking a place of their own. Soon the Park was settled by nearly 800 people primarily of African Descent. Initially a few whites, primarily from Hungary and other Eastern European countries, had moved into this area as well, but by the mid 1950's It had become and overwhelmingly African American community and without knowledge or perhaps because of the desire to have a place of our own, black people began to move out from Cleveland and settled in the area. This community was soon settled by nearly 800 people of primarily African descent. There were initially a few whites primarily from Hungary and other Eastern European countries that moved into this area as well, but by the mid 1950's, it had become a mainly African American community.

My Grandparents, Luke and Genie Walker moved from Cleveland with their nine children to Chagrin Falls Park in October 1929, just a few days before the stock market crash and the beginning of the great depression. They had been living in a railroad car down in the freight yards in Cleveland, so for them this was an opportunity of a lifetime.

Several years later, my parents Felton and Lula Hitchcock married and raised their family in the Park. They had six children, my brothers Felton Jr.; George; Milton; William and their only girl, my sister Florine.

I share with you this background to identify the milieu in which I was born and lived until I relocated to Philadelphia, Pa at the age of 19 years. For my first nineteen years, life was an amazingly wondrous adventure created by fields, streams, creeks, amazement and family. One, of a secure family, with religious training, a good education and exposure to man's inhumanity to man as witnessed on any given weekend in this community, when hope and promise gave way to stress, alcohol and bar brawls.

It was a place where any child would have been glad to grow up and from which any child would have taken an understanding of opportunity and immense possibility from a world that belongs to those who are not afraid to venture out, to explore and find ones niche in life.

While I did not have anything to do with where I came into this world, I fully enjoyed growing up in this way. Whatever hardships we endured as a result of this upbringing such as; no sidewalks or paved streets, with outdoor toilets and carrying water from a well, I didn't feel as if I suffered any deprivation, instead I feel honored and very grateful to the people that chose Chagrin Falls Park as their community. They have provided me with guidance, love and direction which have served me well as an adult.

The word "chagrin" means (Disappointment). The word, however, is not at all representative of the town that bares its name. It is in no way a disappointing place in which to live. I can only imagine that it is so named because of the waterfalls around which the town was built. On both sides of the wrought iron bridge that divides the town, the falls spring forth and cascades about fifty feet down to the rocks. While it provides an echo effect, which I am sure in some way confused the first settlers into thinking that it was a much deeper and steeper drop and so I can only conceive that to be the origin of the name chagrin, when they finally arrived at the falls, their disappointment must have been palpable.

This area of Northeastern Ohio is one of the classically beautiful areas of the country and is ripe with fields, streams, wooded areas that reflect open spaces and panoramic views. The village of Chagrin Falls and its' neighbor Chagrin Falls Park, while similarly named could not be more different demographically, or economically.

Chagrin Falls is a town of about 5000 people, 100% European Americans, which at one point was listed as one of the ten richest communities in the United States and is home to Professionals with six and seven figure incomes. Chagrin Falls Park is a working class section of approximately 800 people, all African Americans with most of them relatives of other families in the community.

Chagrin Falls Park was a very homogeneous community, because it had to be. Surrounded by adversaries on all sides, the residents had, largely, to rely upon their own ingenuity and that of their neighbors in the community.

Early in the history of the development of Chagrin Falls Park saw members of the community awake to the firelight of a burning cross.

This would set the stage for the inharmonious and contentious relationship between these two communities, that to a certain degree remains the prominent manor in which the two communities interrelate today, but in a much more subtle yet equally as devastating fashion.

For this first time, these residents found out why the lots had been offered at such a low price, but decided in a community meeting that they would stay and build a life for their families. At this point the depression was in full swing and that combined with the problem of the Klu Klux Klan, Latin for circle of friends meant that it would be impossible to sell their properties and so it was incumbent upon them to make the best of a bad situation, and so they settled down to building their homes, planting gardens, building churches and setting up schools.

Compare this with a slow moving pace, framed with ponds, horses, polo fields, fishing and tourism and you have a very incongruous setting. These are some of the factors that led to the mental cauldron, which produced this book.

As I have grown into adulthood and traveled extensively throughout Africa, I am struck by the consistency with which the majority population, and by that I mean the Europeans who colonized America, and other Countries in Africa, like South Africa and Namibia, I am struck by the similarities in how they are set up and organized to serve a certain populace.

Chagrin Falls Park could have been superimposed with Soweto in South Africa or Windhoek, Namibia West Africa. The significant thing about this in my mind, is that those populations had to fight an armed struggled to gain their rights. I know that there are some significant differences between their struggles and ours here in America, but the prospect needs to be at least examined, if only from a sociological perspective, to perhaps determine whether without it, African Americans as a group will be respected and their rights enforced.

To all of those who have ever called Chagrin Falls Park home I dedicate this book of poems, reveries, short stories and musings.

HOME ROOM

The year was 1960, the year that I and my fellow Black students entered into the freshman class at Kenston High School. Indeed, it was a cultural shock for all involved. While relationships between the two groups sometimes seemed as if they were cordial, all too often the underlying tension would boil to the surface. This was one of those times, and the school would never be the same again.

Friction has been building in the Park for some time as the result of what was perceived as the continued abuse and degradation of the community by the majority Chagrin Falls community, in what we felt was collusion between County Administrators and School Board Officials, which has started more than three decades prior.

As the result of these totally unacceptable policies, which totally ignored the will and desires of this minority community the status quo was no longer acceptable. Because of the stance taken by the School Board of Geauga County, the residents of Chagrin Falls Park, affectionately referred to by its residents as "The Park" had decided to build their own school in the community and hire teachers from Cleveland, to travel from Cleveland every day out to the community and teach their children.

Tension was extremely high in the classroom this morning as, students, teachers, and administrators anticipated trouble. I sat at my desk near the back of the room full of excitement, yet at the same time filled with the dread of what my parents would say and do, if I got into trouble. I had been at Kenston High School for only a few months, and this would definitely be the most momentous day since my arrival here.

My parents would always say to me "boy we didn't send you to school to be a trouble maker, we sent you to school to get an education." But today was different. There had been talk all weekend long about the racial tension that was pervasive in the school. We were determined to do something about it.

It had been thirty years since blacks went to go to high school in an all white community. Blacks in nineteen twenty nine had begun to buy property in the Ohio County of Geauga, and the racial tension came with the purchase. However, the discriminatory behavior of the townsfolk, for the most part, had been tolerated, with only minor, sporadically occurring incidents.

The truth be told, the thing that kept contentiousness to a minimum between the two groups was the fact the black community was self-contained, limiting contacts between the communities groups. The Whites owned and controlled most everything in the county. With the black population being less than five percent of the total population, we were relegated to the backwoods of the social strata.

This day, the Black students, in this predominantly white school, had decided that it was time to take a stand. The feeling of foreboding, mixed with elation and fear, encased the student body like a fourth dimension. It had been determined, primarily by the black students themselves, without consulting any adults, that there would be a demonstration.

A sit in, was planned and implemented over the grading system, which effectively denied all black students any semblance of fairness. This policy had to be protested. To let it stand would be the height of hypocrisy and against every principle that we had been taught as students at Chagrin Falls Park Elementary.

In a meeting between the principal Mr. Bachelor and the 40 black students, the principal had made it clear that there was some outrage by white parents. Some parents, in the white community felt that black students should not be graded on the same scale as white students, because in some way would reduce the standing of the school.

It had been arbitrarily decided that black students could not, and would not be graded on the same scale as the white students.

The decision was made that regardless of what grades I received, or the other thirty nine Black students received on papers, test,, home work and Class participation, even if you were consistently performing at an A or B level, the highest grade that you could receive on you report card was a C, and that under exceptional circumstances, you could be given a C +.

Needless to say, this, had not been received well by the black students, but most of the white students thought that it was justified. The scene was set for a showdown and for the first time the black students decided amongst themselves, to stand up for their rights.

Because of continued abuse and degradation on the part of the majority community, this includes, administrator, teachers, and other elected officials in the school district, This has all started over a decade ago, when as the result of an unacceptable policy of totally ignoring the educational needs off the children of Chagrin Falls Park , on the part of the School Board of Geauga County, the County in which Chagrin Falls was located, the residents of Chagrin Falls Park, affectionately known by its residents as "The Park" had decided to build their own school in the community and hire teachers from Cleveland, to travel from Cleveland every day out to the community to teach the kids.

The community of Chagrin Falls Park is adjacent to the City of Chagrin Falls, Ohio. They somehow ended up in different counties and because of, in my opinion gerrymandering; they have two separate and distinct school systems and governing authorities.

The redistricting was no accident and paralleled on many levels, the racial animus of the day, and that which continues to be in place to this day. Children from the Park are not allowed to go to local schools and have to be bussed 45 minutes, to a school that is literally surrounded by farmland and cattle. This indignity sat none too well with the residents of Chagrin Falls Park, and was a seething cause of disagreement between the two populations.

About eight years before and after numerous meetings between the School Board and the residents had resulted only in wasted time and spent energy, the people got together and had built a one room, school house, that held grades one through seven. This was its first graduating class.

The people back then, working together raised money, hired builders and pitched in as a community. They worked tirelessly for months, men, women and children, until we had a school of our own. It was a real community effort, with the Cleveland Grand Lodge of the Prince Hall Mason, providing, material, financial and logistical help to build this community school. It was a great success, and it was then that the residents new they had a very special community.

There were many talented Black builders, masons and other that had decided to move out to The Park, after having purchased property from a Jewish newspaper man who had purchased 110 acres of property adjacent to the quaint town of Chagrin Falls, upon which he had hoped to construct summer homes, but had been forced to rethink his purchased, and led him to hatch a scheme to sell the property to unsuspecting blacks who he knew would jump on the offer. In addition, I believe he saw this as a way of the paying back the residents of Chagrin Falls, who had treated him with such hostility and Anti-Semitism. In the final analysis he figured that he would show them, and he did.

The Park for the first couple of decades was a veritable wasteland, with muddy trails for streets, no running water or electricity. The was rural living at its finest, but the more people moved out to The Park, the more the infrastructure started to be laid that would eventually form a hamlet of nearly 800 people with paved roads, running water and all the amenities of home.

The residents of The Park had come to stay, and regardless of the burning crosses and the strange death of some of the residents the people of the Park had banded together to build themselves quite a community. The homes, to a large extent were not built up to any code and were quite often gerryrigged, but for some it was the first real home they had known sense leaving the south.

The great depression, while not in full effect on the country as a whole, had been the normal state of affairs for large numbers of Black people. My grandparents included.

Prior to moving from Cleveland, my grandparents Luke and Genie Walker had lived in a railroad car, somewhere near down Cleveland and had call that railroad car home for nearly four years. They, like many others jumped at the opportunity to own some land of their own, even if was measured in lots and not acres.

When the add first appeared in the Cleveland Spectator, there had been a rush to purchase the $5.00 lots, never realizing the reason behind the opportunity to purchase this property was to be part of a cruel hoax, a payback that would have echoes of Jim crow for the newest residents of the area, that sought only a chance to start a new future and live out the American dream. The dream had rapidly deteriorated into a nightmare.

The construction of the school had been a roaring success and so from there, there was no turning back. Backwards Never, Forward Ever they sang at community meetings. The school, when it was completed a few weeks later, was named Chagrin Falls Park Elementary School.

As the result of pressure from the community, the school district of Bainbridge, which is the township in were the community is located, decided that they would provide used books and equipment to the school, but that once the children graduated from Elementary school they would then transfer to Kenston High, the County High School.

Ours was the first class to go from this all black school, Park Elementary, to an all white high school. The key to remember is that the teachers who taught at the elementary school taught the achievements and contributions from People of Color, especially African Americans in all walks of life. There were some exceptionally bright students of color, who came out of Chagrin Falls Park Elementary School and would not be denied access to a quality education.

My grandparents (The Walkers) had moved out to Chagrin Falls, Ohio in 1929 as the third black family in the area. My mother, along with five sisters and four brothers had been brought out to the country from Cleveland as young children and had been raised right in this community. By the late 1930's, the community had grown to over 100 families, with over 700 people; over 25% of them are related to me. Growing up for me in Chagrin Falls Park was a test of survival and ingenuity.

As a child, I was surrounded by trees; horse farms; orchards; ponds, Churches and relatives. The days were filled with fun, culture, history, sports and the accomplishments of a too often neglected group of people, African Americans.

I started school at Chagrin Falls Park Elementary and as one of the first students to go through the community school for the entire seven grades; I had been identified by the school as a bright and promising student. I was an honor student and graduated from the first grade as the salutatorian, giving a speech to the gather community in my white cap and gown, at the tender age of seven.

I have never forgotten the elation, which I felt combined with the sheer terror of be speaking in front of the community. My cousin Robert (crow) Watson was the valedictorian and together we had been designated as the brightest students in the class and it stayed that way through the entire seven years at Park Elementary.

The first year of the school was perhaps the best, as there was so much excitement in the community among the students that attended the school. In addition to the building which sat in the middle of the community, there was a playground with swings, slides, merry-go-rounds and later a basketball court that for the teenagers in the community was the center of attraction. All life occurred on the playground, between the ages of six years old until the late teen-age years.

In addition to the social events and community meetings that were held at the Community Center, it also became the cultural hub, when during the spring events, plays, concerts and community business would be conducted from stages and rostrums built for such presentations.

The community of Chagrin Falls Park was hidden away amongst the trees and if you were not aware of its existence, you would easily drive right by it. I remember on a number of occasions when the community attempted to identify itself by placing a sign at the end of Woodland Avenue, which was the official entrance to the community, only to find it torn down and into pieces the next morning by the forces in the community who did not want to see this community in any way linked to the affluent while community of Chagrin Falls. Chagrin Falls was perennially listed in the top ten wealthiest communities in America.

In between burning crosses, derogatory remarks on the sidewalk, the lack of access to jobs in the area and much more, the residents of Chagrin Falls Park managed to eke out living and to grow families. They also managed to educate their children and to live out a portion of the

American dream. It was to some extent, a wonderful place to grow up in, because of its bucolic nature.

The adults made sure that there was activity for the kids and a sound upbringing in the church. Families were, by and large stable, with incidents of abuse and alcoholism, combined with baseball games, Friday night dances, swimming in the pond, hopping the train during the summer to ride to the blackberry fields, where you could pick some of the biggest and most savory blackberries every uncovered on earth. These were, soon turned, by my mother, into the most delicious blackberry cobblers ever eaten.

Mark twain would have given up life on the Mississippi and felt right at home in the confines of Chagrin Falls Park Nestled in the Chagrin Valley, where over two hundred years before tribes of Native Americans had flourished, leaving behind numerous arrowheads and other artifacts of living.

Today, however, Chagrin Falls stands as a tourist attraction, where large numbers of tourist take in the bucolic view, while savoring the ice cream served at the shop located above the falls which divides this quaint little town. The road past the ice cream shop, Franklin Street, runs about a mile more north right past the entrance to Chagrin Falls Park. Depending on the timing, there may or may not be a sign, denoting its existence.

There was also a turn of the century paper mill still in operation, which provided a few jobs to the residents of Chagrin Falls Park. Over the years and still to today there are racial tensions in this corner of American, based upon the lack of fairness in the treatment of these residents of Chagrin Falls Park, Ohio.

The community of Chagrin Falls Park is approximately one half mile from the heart of its wealthy neighbor Chagrin Falls, Ohio, but there is the difference between, literally black and white, in most major aspects of the two communities.

Little did I know that this morning in homeroom would begin one of the most eventful days of my young life to this point? Mrs. Hurd, my English teacher, also doubled as the homeroom teacher. Teachers throughout the school had been warned to be alert and to report any potential for violence, or any sign of weapons.

Anticipating trouble, I had brought with me a chisel about five inches in length and sharp, which I had made in metal shop the year before. I had intended to take it out of my bag and put it into my locker, but as fate would have it, I had forgotten. When I pulled my books out of the bag, out, unceremoniously fell the chisel. The noise that it made, to me sounded like a cacophony of rushing sound, which for that single moment, took my breath away, a moment which put me temporarily in a state of suspended animation.

With all eyes now focused on me, I proceeded to pick the chisel up, as nonchalantly as I possibly could and put it back into my bag, but with my stomach on the floor, I could not possibly imagine what was to follow.

After leaving homeroom, and on the way to my next class, Algebra, I stopped at my locker and put the chisel inside, but the damage had been done. After approximately, 30 minutes in the class, the door opens and in comes the Principal, I believe it was Mr. Hettinger at the time, He motioned that I should come out into the hallway. I was petrified, and immediately had this sense of foreboding. What would my Mother and Father think?

As I stepped out into the hallway, with just a brief glance over my shoulder at the students remaining in the room, I knew from the look on their faces that this was not going to be school as usual. Not, for me, nor for anyone else that was a part of the school system or either of these communities. As the door to the classroom, closed two large Deputy Sheriffs immediately surrounded me. After looking through my bag, they escorted me to my locker, where while searching through my belongings, they found the chisel.

I was immediately escorted to the Principals office, where I overheard the Principal on a phone call to my home, talking with my mother and telling her that they were arresting me and taking me up to the county jail. The charge was inciting violence.

It was then that I realized the meaning of the phrase "I wish I was dead. At the time, I did not know that my cousin, Alvin Walker had gotten into a fight with someone in his homeroom a few moments before my chisel fell out of my bag. Agreeably, the sentiment on the part of the administration was that this is a very delicate situation, which it was, and that they needed to get control of it before it boiled over into a full-scale riot in classrooms throughout the school. In this climate, I became the scapegoat, and was perceived by the administration, as the perfect example to be made, on their part. Fate has strange ways of pushing one to the fore.

Even thought my cousin had actually been in a fight, was of no consequence, because it was fist to fist, even though the two combatants were of different racial groupings, it was felt that the worst punishment, that they could levy upon the two of them, was a three day suspension.

I, on the other hand, was arrested, and taken to jail. One of the things that most remains with me from that day, is the fact that my cousin lived right next door to me, which meant that when the Police took him home and because we were in the same police car, I got to see my home, but was totally unable to go in. I wondered briefly, at the not so tender age of thirteen, whether or not I would ever see my parents or my home again.

I sat transfixed in the back of the police car, with two Sheriffs Deputies, both white, (as there were and I believe this still holds true today that there are no black police officers in Geauga County) sat up in the front.

Not much has changed. Between the two Deputies and myself was a wire mesh grate, ostensibly to protect the Deputies from their charges lodged in a tight space in the back of the patrol car. I managed to muffle my sobs, but I was on full blown sob alert inside, as this was my first experience with the justice system. Fortunately they would be few and far between.

One of the things that I had always loved about this part of the country was the scenery, which in the fall was without question the most spectacular display of color that one could ever imagine. The beauty of the surroundings was in noticeable contrast to my spirit as I rode this lonely road to Geauga Jail.

Little did I know that I would spend the next three days in a jail cell, which was for all intents and purposes, to me the equivalence of a coffin.

A part of me died during that three days and was buried forever that afternoon. Fortunately I managed, in spite of this, to grow into adulthood, with a healthy sense of self and able to easily overcome the scars of this incident.

When I arrived at the jail, I was first booked with photos being taken and my fingerprints. Everyone seemed to know what was going on in the building and were looking at me as if I had plotted to assassinate the President of the United States or something.

After this I was lead to a small cell, just off the main section of the jail and placed in a cell about six by ten feet. I will never forget as the door to the cell closed behind me. This was the first time I had not been able to move about freely, and it really hit home. After a few minutes, I began to cry uncontrollably. I don't remember calling for my mother, but if I didn't it was only because I was crying so hard.

At thirteen years old I had arrived at the place that I had been warned so often, not to go. I was alone and this was the worst part of the entire episode. I anticipated that someone from the family would soon be coming to get me, or at lease to see how I was. I even half thought that I would be released within a few hours. This was quickly dispelled and day turned into night. As darkness fell, I realized that my imagination would be very important to making it through this ordeal.

I was served a couple of sandwiches, an apple and some orange juice for dinner. Following the meal I cried myself to sleep and didn't wake up until the next morning. No one came for me that night, not the next day, nor the next day. For three days I was held essentially incommunicado. No visitors, no lawyers and no family. It was horrible. I believe that I made up my mind then that incarceration was not for me. If the objective of this was to scare me straight, they did that even before the concept was invented.

I vowed, that evening, that this was the last time I would go to jail. Whatever I had to do would be done on this side of the law. Oh well, the best laid plans of mice and men, do sometimes go awry. I would subsequently be the guess at some of the finer establishments in our country overnight for traffic tickets and things of that nature, but never again was I faced with the dread that I experienced that night.

The first morning dawned sunny and bright and I was sure that today would bring about my release, and If not I was sure that I would see my parents. Neither happened, but what did happen was what I believe actually saved my sanity. I was unaware at that age of any laws which forbade the law from keeping a minor locked up, without an attorney, a phone call, or any real explanation as to what I was being charged with and what exactly my rights were under these circumstances. This after all is long before Miranda.

I guess it should have been expected with the high level of racial animus that existed during those days in the County of Geauga and throughout Ohio during that period. I was left at the tender age of thirteen to pretty much fend for myself. That is until David Dawes, who had sat next to me in one of my classes was brought in and put in my cell. David, who is white, had been one of the few whites in the school that had seemed somewhat different and didn't appear to be overtly racist.

I must admit that I was glad to see him. For that matter I was glad to see anyone with whom I could chat, and pass the countless hours between boredom and sobbing. David was experienced with the system and had been arrested earlier in the day at school with a switchblade knife, which he maintained he carried all the time, and did not have it specifically for the situation now boiling over at the school.

He calmly explained to me that as a juvenile, I would be out in no time because the law forbids the holding of youth for prolonged periods without council. The key was that the law allowed you to hold a minor if he was a potential danger to himself or to someone else. That is how I had been classified. They really wanted to set an example with me and I would have to endure two more days of incarceration. Fortunately David was with me through the ordeal, and managed to be released only after I did. We became friends after we both returned to school, but that is another story.

David managed to talk one of the people in the office at the jail out of a deck of cards and so at least we had something to occupy our time between meals, crying and sleeping.

It was actually nice to have him as company, as it gave me my first opportunity to get to know someone of another race. It was the first time that I had a sleep over with a white person. It was not what I would have asked for nor expected, but that was one of the benefits of that time in jail. I only realized this many years later.

Finally after nearly three days of incarceration, I heard my name being called "Anderson Hitchcock" you're going home. Get your things together . . . By this time I had an opportunity to say goodbye to David and then the guard was at the door with the keys. That was one of the greatest sounds that I ever heard. I momentarily felt bad for David, but was soon overcome with the thought of being free, or at least being out of jail. Freedom is definitely a relative term, which I would learn much later on, through meditation and travel. Freedom is indeed a state of mind.

At thirteen, however, my mind was on getting out of there as fast as I possibly could. When I rounded the corridor into the main area of the Sherriff's Department, there was my Mother and Father standing looking quite stern and not amused at all. I tried not to show too much excitement and to act as if it had been only a minor inconvenience, but before I could reach them I burst into tears. I didn't think I had more tears left, as I had cried almost continuously since hearing the cell door close behind me.

With my mother and father was a white gentleman that I did not know, but my mother introduced him to me as the lawyer who had managed to get me out of the joint. I found out that I had been released under my own recognizance, but would have to appear in court on Saturday, where it would be determined what my punishment would be for the crime of carrying a concealed weapon, with intent to do bodily harm. On the contrary, it was my body that I was worried about being harmed. The chisel in my mind was for self defense.

Unfortunately, when Saturday came and we went before the Judge he didn't share my sentiment and the sentence was not what I wanted to hear, but it could have been worse. As I left the jail with my parents and the attorney, I had a new sense of who; I was as a person and what my values were. That incident definitely helped to mold me into the man I became, but set me on the road to question, what justice is. An answer for which I am still searching.

Ride home was interminable and very quiet. No one spoke, accept my mother a couple of times to ask how I was doing, and whether I was hungry or not. My mother was always so kind and caring, that it made whatever my father thought or had to say of little significance. It was clear that he would act out of anger and lash out, and so that is what I expected. That is not what I got from him and it was surprising. After we arrived home and my brothers and sister had their fill of mocking me and laughing at my predicament, I was called into my parents bed room and after being scolded for taking the chisel to school, my father stood up and for the first and last time in my memory gave me a big hug.

That was the first and only time I ever remember my father hugging me. I felt good and reassured, and I still savor the memory of that embrace until today.

On the way out of the bedroom my mother told me to get something to eat, take a bath and get ready to go to choir practice. I was shocked the last thing I wanted to think about was being humiliated by going to choir practice, where all of my classmates would be waiting, most of the young people from the church went to the school knew what had happened. I dreaded the thought of going to Youth Choir practice, but my mother insisted, so I had little choice but to suck it up and go.

Little did I know what reception awaited me at the Church. Things had taken an unexpected turn at the school since I had gone to jail, and the situation had been resolved in a most unexpected way. When I walked into the Church, practice had already begun. The choir was singing one of my favorite songs, so I decided not to interrupt, but to wait until they had finished this number. There was no one in the vestibule but me. The song that they were singing was "His Eye is on the Sparrow".

The song gave me a great deal of comfort and I realized that even in jail the Lord provides for our every need. This is a lesson that would serve me well throughout my life, up to this day; I believe this to be the case and I adopted my own unique version of that concept. I often say "Life is Good and God" is better. He certainly proved that to me that night.

As the song ended and I walked into the Church and everyone burst into applause and gave me a standing ovation. I was totally and utterly surprise, as I was prepared for almost anything but that. I later found out the applause was for the fact that there had been a reversible by the Principal and the School Board , that everyone, regardless of race, creed or color would be able to compete on their merits and would receive that grade that they had earned through their hard work and perspiration. Needless to say I was floored, but happily so.

Not until after choir practice did I learn, that the white students had staged a sit in of their own the day after I went to jail, because they felt that the rule was unjust and didn't allow them to compete with us on an equal basis. It was an amassing turn of events, which I had never anticipated. The white students felt that it would be competition that would prepare everyone for what was ahead academically and that where competition is prescribed by a color line everyone would suffer.

The Principal had rescinded his order and everyone, once again was encouraged to do the best work that they could and let the chips fall where they may. With professional parents and with access to the best education that money could buy the students were not concerned and as a result felt that they would be denied equally under this rule as would the Black students.

While racial animus on campus didn't disappear entirely there was an atmosphere of competition was healthy and mutually rewarding. It was a great victory for tolerance and understanding, and a most heartfelt lesson for yours truly.

Saturday came, and with me in tow my parents trudged up to the Geauga Courthouse in Chardon, Ohio, which is about an hour from our home. In order not to be late, we decided to leave early, and were there when our attorney arrived. He was professional enough and warned my parents that the sentence could be anything from probation to time in jail. I thought to myself, time in jail, oh no. Just then the attorney indicated that he had submitted a writ to have me put on probation, and to get off with time served.

As we entered the chamber of the Judge, everyone was already in place, and we took our seats. The judge asked a few questions of me, such as; what is my interest, and had I ever carried a weapon to school before. I answered no to the latter and told him that I was interested in sports and hoped to play basketball, football and run track. He indicated that if I were to be sentenced for this infraction, it would prohibit my ability to play organized sports, but that he was going to give me another chance. The words came to me like a bolt of lightning and penetrated my soul. I was overjoyed just at the words. I hadn't even heard the complete sentence yet, but already I felt a sense of relief.

The Judge went on to sentence me to one year probation, where my parents would have to bring me to a probation officer once per month, to keep up with my progress towards staying out of trouble. I knew this would be somewhat of a burden to my parents, but the Judge indicated that if they could not bring me, then one of my uncles or aunts could bring me. My parents thanked the Judge and that was it.

The attorney as it had turned out was the employer of my Aunt Ella and had agreed to represent me pro bono, which means without cost. I learned that it is not something they did often.

I am not sure my parents would have been able to raise the money, but fortunately for me, we didn't have to find out. That, I believe partly explains, why my parents didn't go ballistic on me when I got out of jail.

I returned to school the next day and was asked by the homeroom teacher Mrs. Hurd to say a few words. The only thing that came to my mind, were these words "Life is Good and God is Better".

HAVE YOU HEARD THE SIDEWALK CRICKET SING

He sings of these and many things

Of life and death

And all in between

He rubs his legs

To get your attention

Then speaks of things

Too numerous to mention

Have you heard the sidewalk cricket sing

He sings of these and many things

Of concrete graves

Where many lie

Of youthful fate

Too young to die

He sings of crimes

Black on Black type

Committed by those

Who fell for the hype

Have you heard the sidewalk cricket sing

He sings of these and many things

Of night near dawn

When silence rings

To remind us of another day

That has faded into time

And passed away

A song

That unwed mothers' play

On jukeboxes

Down alleys

Where the homeless lay

A song

So clear

So crisp

So gay

A chorus of his cronies

Wail away

Intoning rhythms of Miles and Byrd

And new sounds of artist

Yet unheard

Have you heard the sidewalk cricket sing

He sings of these and many things

Of smoke filled bars

And bombed out cars

Places filled with fear

As last, call for alcohol

They don't like to hear

He sings

Of Poets

Of Pimps

And of Prostitutes

Of old recluses

In second hand suits

Wearing shoes from Stacy Adams

But to them

It really doesn't matter

As from the cold

They shake and shutter

As their lives

Run down the sidewalk

Into the gutter

Have you heard the sidewalk cricket sing

He sings of these and many things

SMALL TOWN AMERICA

Small town America

Cascaded waters roar

Beneath iron bridges

Along main streets

Passed curio shops

Activity laden

While bright bulbed

Bundles of joy

Serve omnipresent spirits

Quaint as an attitude

You sit

Gazebo like

A lone sentinel

Posted

On the outskirts

Of Middle America

Proudly playing revile

On the bugle of tradition

Small town America

Where no one knows hunger

Yet, everyone senses starvation

Disappointing

You are not

In all aspects

Save humanity

You found steamy

Lush valleys

While treasure hunters among you

Still seek solemn devotion

At the altar of

Antique

Oriental BMW's

Small town America

Petrified

Mortified

Yuppified

Save your beauty

For generations

LAY LIGHTLY ON THE CONCRETE

Lay lightly on the

Creep gently through the dirt

Planting cement beds of flowers

Mixed with fallow blood drenched earth

Lay lightly on the concrete

Casting pillows made with brick

Then sleep

The sleep of eternity

One never can predict

Lay lightly on the concrete

Forging blankets out of steel

To cover and protect those

Whom God no longer will

Lay lightly on the concrete

SEA OF REALITY

I am lost on a sea of reality

With light so bright

Its' blinding to my sight

My sails were strung high

And pointed toward the sky

But there was no wind on this sea of reality

Life's maze I couldn't gauge

For the storms

That did rage

Upon this sea of reality

What sun that did shine

Came out only with the wine

To warm this sea of reality

I am left without oar

Too far from either shore

To drift eternally

Upon this sea of reality

KOI

Koi, like man Travels

From first day of life till end

Without leaving pond

UNREQUITED LOVERS

Was during ocean tides

I started to surmise

That the beauty of your kiss

Was once found on nature's lips

Seldom seen

Drops of dew

Exchanged

Between me and you

Formless clouds

Cloak our eyes

As waves of truth

Fall and rise

Gliding over

Lather

Loam

They ride

The current

To some

Far off home

Where Quixotic

Tuffs of form

Continually lap the shore

And windmills tilt no more

Passions of the heart

Repeatedly gnaw

Like rodents

On artificial cheese

Stifling summer's heat

Obscuring evening's breeze

My lance drawn

I charge the summit

Planting poetries flag atop

In memoriam

While overlooking

Anderson Hitchcock

Fallow fields

Where

Unrequited lovers

To this day

Ly there

Silent

Still.

SIRENS IN THE NIGHT

Screaming

Screeching

Sirens Wailing

Blaring

Blurting

New Peaks

In need of scaling

Beads of Sweat

On my forehead glistening

As to the high pitched

Piercing sound

I am continually listening

Drenching

Dangling

Darting

Reminders of an impossible past

Aghast with rhyme and rhythm

While attempting to penetrate

This nocturnal prism

Drifting

Drooling

Dreaming

Emanating

Curious growls

Of cajoling slumber

Slowing sliding

Slippery slopes

Into crevices of little hope

Lay I huddled hideously in fetaled

Fright

From frequent squealing

Of death white

Sirens in the night

THE HARLEM TO LEIMERT PARK CONVENTION

African tribes in America

Do hereby declare our intention

In this Harlem to Leimert Park Convention

To protect the rights

Of indigenous Americans

Of African descent

Who have for over four hundred years

Paid rent

Must now inform you

Through this griot

Musician

Town crier

That the mortgage

We do hereby retire

Reclaiming full ownership

Of our lives

We have paid the ultimate price

For a cornerstone to be laid

Upon the heels of America's heart

Done more that our part

Been loyal to a fault

Some would say

Home is where

When you go

You have a right to stay

They must take you in

Yet, here we have been made to feel

Uncomfortable

Synonymous with sin

At best

At worse

As if cursed

African Tribes in America

Do hereby declare our intention

In this Harlem to Leimert Park Convention:

The first right is:

The right to self-defense against all enemies; foreign; domestic; governmental, organizational; or fraternal.

The second right is:

The right to be totally involved in our governance.

The third right is:

The right to create wealth, to be used upon behalf of all oppressed people throughout the world.

The fourth right is:

The right to be totally self-determinant about what our rights are.

We hereby declare these intentions in this Harlem to Leimert Park Convention.

THE BROWN PAPER BAG

The Brown Paper Bag

The Brown Paper Bag

They put it next to me

To see if I could be

An alpha or a Q

That's what they used to do

It almost broke my heart

They said I was just too dark

They really didn't care

If I put pomade in my hair

They said I would never pass

I said you can kiss my ass

With your brown paper bag

With your brown paper bag

The brown paper bag

The brown paper bag

It really was a drag

They would always boast and brag

Then they would put me on the bench

Right next to Willie Lynch

And the brown paper bag

The brown paper bag

It left its mark on me

As you can clearly see

I am always quite ecstatic

When they ask me paper of plastic

And you know which one I'd choose

Even until today

You can always hear me say

Don't give me

No brown paper bag

No brown paper bag

How can you blame me?

When my own brothers

Would frame me

With the brown paper bag

With the brown paper bag

So the moral of this story

As you'll never have to worry

Because with words I'll never mince

For you ladies and you gents

And your significant others

With the brown paper bag test

You're still aiding Willie Lynch

With his brown paper bag

With his brown paper bag

P.O.W

Black widow

Weaving webs

Of watered down visions

To entangle white and

Callous concepts of the future

While living from day to day

In treasonous epochs

Of false freedom

Compounded by guards

Not limited to lamenting

Labored moans

Of self satisfaction

At our dilemma

Befriended beneath

Harsh outcries

Of inhumanity

Preserved from platitudes

Of old

When black was colored

And the nigra not so bold

Concealing invisible prison camps

Newly built

For even

If the balance

Of life should tilt

The chains could not be broken

For we are given only the stolen

Although through our culture

We have known

That in times we were mighty

It seems now

That we are all

Just

Prisoners **O**f **W**hitey

THE INDOMITABLE BLACK MAN

This mythic phantom

Stalks the forest of our mind

The indomitable Black Man

Only rarely glimpsed

Scavenges amongst the entrails

Of a once powerful empire

Now well past its primal glory

Still he

Remains quite capable

Evading

Capture

Capitulation

Constriction

Extermination

A legendary yeti

Untamed

Yet seldom viewed

In his natural habitat

Instinct

Gives

Structure

To his

Dementia

As he

Crouches

Trembling

Behind bushes

On all four

With

Knuckles

Bleeding

Being drug

Over

The Holy Grail

Of Negritude

While

Darwin's process of

Natural Selection

Plays itself out

In front of his eyes

Cro Magnum

Predators

Prey

Upon the Indomitable Black Man

As he flees

Leaving

Swatches of

Course

Nappy hair

On

Brambles

Thistles of thorn

Cacophonies

Of whispered innuendo

Cultural leeches

Sing out

As they

Seek

To suck

His blood

And

Devour

His flesh

Co-opted

By Otherholism

He is transformed

At the sub-atomic level

And allowed

To blend into

Any background

Whatsoever

The indomitable Black Man

Mild

Mannered

Mainly

Except when cornered

Then he

Explores

Expands

Explodes

Into

Efficacious

Regimes of

Self Inflicted

Corporal punishment

While doing

Mental gymnastics

The indomitable Black Man

Contemplates

Conscripts

Contaminates

Shadows

Silhouetted

Shaped

Against

Darkness's

Backdrop

Upon which is projected

Posters

Trumpeting

Rewards

For the capture

Dead or alive

Of an Indomitable Black Man

Hunters

Remain

Down wind

While preparing

Their traps

And cleaning their weapons

They reminisce

About the good old days

When it was

Always

Open season

On this

Particular quarry

They

Prepare meticulously

To hunt

This illusive

Missing link

Histories

Misanthrope

This mammal

Impregnated

Promiscuously

In wooded enclaves

By supple nymphs

Where

They often

Get lost

While in search of

A creature

That is more myth

Than material

More whispered rumor

Than confirmed fact

More wishful thinking

Than substance adorned

The indomitable Black Man

Prized for his originality

Blames himself

For having tusk

Made of wisdom

Which are

Highly prized by all

Non Africans

Surrounded

Intellectually

By chameleons

In picture frames

Composite photographs

Of their trophies

Mounted

On walls

With

Misguided

Motives of

Machismo

Expressed

Animalistically

Through

Guttural sounds

Anderson Hitchcock

If the indomitable Black Man

Has fallen

Gravely ill

In the forest

Of his mind

But

You can still

Hear his cry

Does this mean

That

He continues

To live and die

As a deaf mute

In the real world

AFFILIATE OF THE GHETTO

Crime

Grime

They both rank high

In the Pantheon

Of Urban Gods

However

I too am an affiliate of the Ghetto

Am I not

Together we stand

Next to statues

Of Lady Liberty

Twirling signs

Spinning

Spitting

Preening

Poised on every street corner

In inner city America

Posing on bus benches

Next to fitties

Energy drinks

I too am an affiliate of the Ghetto

Riding waves of noise

Nauseated by poverty's stench

Strolling naked

Through

Morning's constitution

Having just awoken

Beneath my favorite park bench

Before permeating nostrils

Traveling urban currents

Wafting lazily

On breezes

Fresh from life's bowels

Broken a billion times

Yet repaired rarely

Limping along

Well traveled by-ways

Too poor to pay

Yet too pungent

To fit in easily

I too am an affiliate of the Ghetto

Like drive by shootings

Loud rap music

Street corner vendors

Of all stripes

Selling

Day old peach cobbler

Bean Pie

Gumbo

Salted peanuts

Faded tee shirts

Meanwhile

Wearing coats

Of human waste

Pulled snuggly

Around aging bodies

While collecting

Signatures

On petitions

Long ago

Outdated

In addition

Bloated egos

Dance

Against sinewy rhythms

Confusing images

Giving off mixed signals

Causing instability

With the chaos

They create

I too am an affiliate of the Ghetto

Careening ever

Contributing never

Accepting caricatures

Of myself

Mimicking feedback

Looping fractals

Long ago rewound

Reset scenes to bleed

On movie screens

Reality's show

Slowed down

To half speed

Motioning one to another

Consciousness

Silently blares

Through speakers

Implanting subliminal

Messages

Cleverly placed

Behind omnipresent

Scrawlings

Graffiti

Spurs

Ghetto warriors to mark

Their territory

And to fight

In fierce campaigns

On urban streets

Where the community

Becomes

The real enemy

And every citizen

Becomes a victim

Of the Un-State

I too am an affiliate of the Ghetto

Gaining little

Growing less

Groveling

Amongst plentitude

Marching in parades

Next to pedantic

Clowns

Buffoons in human suites

Laundered

Tailored

Teasing

Tonsorial

Pallids

Perhaps

I too

Have become

An affiliate of the Ghetto

I'VE REACHED MY LIMIT BABY

I've reached my limit baby

And you ain't in it baby

I've reached my limit baby

And you ain't in it baby

You on the outskirts of town

And your vehicle done broken down

But I can't help you baby

No I can't help you baby

I've reached my limit baby

But you ain't in it baby

I've reached my limit baby

And you ain't in it baby

There was a time

It was true

All I wanted was

To be with you

But I've reached my limit baby

And you ain't in it baby

I've reached my limit baby

And you ain't in it baby

I've reached my limit baby

And you ain't in it baby

You're on the outside looking in

And your welcome done worn thin

Cause I've reached my limit baby

And you're not in it baby

I've reached my limit baby

And you ain't in it baby

Now it's time for you to go

And I don't want to see you no more

Cause I've reached my limit baby

And you ain't in it baby

I've reached my limit baby

And you ain't in it baby

Please hang up the phone

Cause from here you're on your own

I've reached my limit baby

But you ain't in it baby

I've reached my limit baby

No you're not in it baby

WE'VE ALWAYS BEEN FREE

We have always been free

Or at least

That's the way it seems to me

Brother man

Busy as can be

Too busy to see

That only the free

Could have survived

These endless heights

Of White hypocrisy

Or weathered the hurricane force

Of global inhumanity

Yes Ma'am

We've always been free

For even as the white flame fades

Into a final flicker

Billions of Black Buds

Blossom beautifully in the sun

For all to see

That we've always been free

Even as we hardened

Hanging from those lynching trees

Rigid as the sea

While black mountains

Rushed into rivers of life

And flowed into streams of eternity

All of this we've endured

For we knew no other way

That we could be

We had to be free

Brought by bondage

Across the ocean

While shackled with chains

Of a constantly violent motion

People!

Think back

Listen to me

Cause while I sat

On my mother's knee

I could feel

The freedom vibrations

Flowing through me

And to my brothers

And to my sisters

Who wait for their turns

To be free

You better

Check out your mentality

Cause you

Sounding mighty slow to me

For we have always been free

At least as free

As we want to be

Freedom! Freedom! Freedom!

RUN NIGGER RUN

Run Nigger

Down Dimly lit hallways

Of hollow whores

Run Nigger

Past piss stained stairs

And processed hairs

Run Nigger

Through shit soaked mire

With death piled higher

Than notes sang

By any choir

Run Nigger

Through the gaping gate

Of this blood drenched hell

You helped to create

While graving bludgeoned bodies

For which you just couldn't wait

Run Nigger

Mixing multitudes

Of minuscule muck

Shuffling stacked decks

Of dick slick niggers

Nefariously nibbling

At nebulous nips of negritude

Smelling roach cooked incense

Of innocent imbecility

Imprinted indelibly

On your mind

Run Nigger

From fascinating fantasies

Of frivolous foxes

Fucking a fistful of fatherless faces

Forcing fearful fits

Of fallow frequency

Run Nigger

To the outstretched arms

And milk white legs

That mean no harm

To lay your head

In the devils bed

Run Nigger Run

THE CORNFIELD

I saw god in a cornfield

Her clotted husk

Clothed her like a cape

The stalk through which

Her essence flowed

Clung with ever deepening

Roots to the newly tilled soil

I saw God in a cornfield

Outside of Cleveland

In the State of Ohio

Upwards ran gray skies

Darkened limbs melted around trees

Hearts were torn and mended

Simultaneously

I saw God in a Cornfield

Outside of Cleveland

In the State of Ohio

The Union of America

Rest upon the broken

Backs of farmers

I saw God in a cornfield

Upon her head

Sat kernels

That shown and sparkled

Superimposing images

Projected through

Lenses

Karmically stained

While cameras

Perched on tripods

Firmly secured in heaven

Photograph

Crow, Mallard, Geese

As they

Feed on her body

Then fly southward for the winter

Imagine as she sits

On her throne

Looks down through the clouds

Clicks the shutter

And smiles

I saw God in a cornfield

Outside of Cleveland

In the State of Ohio

The Union of America

Rest upon the broken backs

Of farmers

I saw God in a cornfield

ZAKIYAH'S POEN (OH DIASPORA)

Excruciating fumes

Infect nostrils

Inhaling racially tinged

Chauvinism

Jamaica to New York

Mimicking mesmerizing waves

Of pungent patois

Oh Diaspora

Saturated lungs

Lance pestilent fantasies

With proverbial fangs

Dripping venom filled

Racial hatred

Into our veins

Surreptitiously

Reinforcing

Inferiorities complex

Through the power of suggestion

Infusing susceptibility

From Johannesburg

To Atlanta

With purely

Illogical reasoning

Cloaked with adulterated animus

Inject pure self-hatred

Through IV drips

Hooked to our subconscious

Oh Diaspora

Particles of doubt

Flow over our brains

Into the core

Of our imagination

Detonating

Divine electrons

Of negativity

As they

Stroll forward

Toward destinies future

Remember the reason

That the gas mask

Was created

Was to protect us

During our journey

Acting as a filter to

The impure thoughts

Of a non human being

Nietzsche's

Discovery

That the shape

Of our skull

Reveals

How much gas

Would need to be released

Into the Chamber of our mind

Auschwitz

Was really

Built for us

Anti-Semitism

Was just

The dress rehearsal

A test run

To perfect the equipment

For racial extermination

Was their

Real motivation

Oh Diaspora

Dominate

Innovate

Alleviate

Anderson Hitchcock

Poverty

First in our minds

Next in the pits

Of our stomachs

Finally in the valley

Of our souls

Oh Diaspora

It is not enough

For me

To love you

You must first

Love yourself

Oh Diaspora

NIGGERITIS

I have Niggeritis

A common fear of niggers

You know

Like Arthritis

Affects the bones

Tonsillitis

Affects the throat

Niggeritis affects the mind

I have Niggeritis

A real fear of niggers

Who through corporations

Pollute the oceans

Foul the air

And spoil the land

I have Niggeritis

An innate weariness

Of niggers who continuously

Wage wars of conquest

Against the entire planet

Swarming like locust

Plundering treasuries

Pillaging coffers of

Petty cash

As a demonstration

Of their superior

Leadership qualities

With Spartan intellect

They rail

Against the poor

I have Niggeritis

A form of Capitalism

Whose bastard progeny

Continually

Moralize against

Saggy pants youth

As a rational fear of

All things nigger

Where

Even the word

Nigger

Triggers

Tryptophan fears

And sensations

Radiate through

Cerebral cortexes

Condition complimentarity

To face inward

And mirror

Itself to infinity

Where Quantifiable truth

Observe obscure fragments

Of puzzle pieces

Marking positions

Placed imprecisely in space

Paintings hang

Askew

In demented

Dimensions

Of human relationships

Which suffer

From

Malaria

Induced maladies

With symptoms

Much worst

Than the

Original disease

Darwin says

Everything

Evolves beyond

Itself

As the spectrum of failure

Subsides

To be replaced

By Inspiration

Which occupies

It's rightful positioned

Atop the apex of reason

Niggeritis trumpets

The fall of Greco Roman logic

Heralding the arrival

Of the seven Plagues

Fear

Fretting

Fornication

Fatalism

Frozen embryos

Fetid ids

And fractured egos

Anderson Hitchcock

Our trepidation

Rides benigness

A Trojan horse

As religion

Sharpens

The hidden dagger

Of the assassin

Philosophy

THE MASTER PHYSICIAN

I stand before you

In awe today

Of the great prescription

Written by the Master Physician

Who heals all

Toil and strife

And replaces it

With a waterfall of peace

Which flows

Throughout for life

It renews the spirit

And soothes the soul

It warms the heart

With embers of spiritual coal

The hearth once stoked

Will never die out

For The Master Physician

Has removed

All misery and doubt

So when you're asked about

The world or the weather

Always repeat

"Life is Good

And God is Better"

And remember

When you see

Smiles plastered

Over their faces

That surely

They are not of these places

On this you can surely bet

That they have made their decisions

And to make spiritual transitions

In order to fill

Their own prescriptions

So long ago

Written by the Master Physician

So if you have pain

Deep down inside

The kind from which

No man or woman

Can hide

Then rather than to

Wail or to moan

Instead

Just throw back your head

Take a dose

Of the medicine

Prescribed by

The Master Physician

Who heals the most

Better than

Any herb

Ever discovered

Is for us

His blood

With which

He has willingly covered

Pearls of wisdom

Written on

His prescription pad

And left to posterity

Were these words

Health Wealth Prosperity

So upon this note

You might contemplate

And Remember

You always have the option

To fill your prescription

So long ago

Written

By the Master Physician

WHY WILLOW TREES WEEP

Willow trees weep

For the souls of black folks

Bones scattered across the sea

They mourn for the

Plight of ancestors

Black like you

And me

Willow trees hang

With the

Weight of centuries

Suspended from

Furrowed brow

Weeping wailing

Gnashing of teeth

Hands kept to eternities plow

Hearts bowed

With gracious majesty

To all who came before

Who struggled

But would never accept

Scorn ridicule or more

Bitter fruit of the poisonous vine

Blossoms at midnight

Battered beaten

Beyond recognition

Illuminated by torches light

Baring witness to the past

While paying homage to the future

Caravans meander

Along nomadic trails

While circles of friends gather

In merriment and mirth

The earth meanwhile trembles

Mankind gives madness birth

Wails, catcalls

A moaning dirge

Cease no more to whine

Willow trees weep

For the age of innocence

Long dead shriveled

On the vine

They weep for the gray haired mother

Whose eyes look on in dread

While her children

Are sold into slavery

Not more to be suckled, fed

Crowded hulls of slave ships

Filled with dankness galore

Humanities soul

Uprooted

For not a clue

Save profit

Save greed

Save selfish vile rumor

Willow trees weep

For the color purple

For fields

For streams and more

They weep

For the Sunday sermon

That gives

Faith

Hope

Joy

They weep for the lash

For boot hill

Castration

And relentless subjugation

All of these things

We've made it through

Anderson Hitchcock

Have you ever seen

A willow tree weep

Or heard its mournful cry

If you have

You know

That willow trees weep

For the souls of black folks

That have died

THE HOURGLASS POET

I am the hourglass poet

Letting words slip through my lips

Like sand through the hourglass of time

Configuring sentences

Into galaxies

Ageless universes

Arise and explode

Into constellations

I am the hourglass poet

Creating contrasting

Concepts of cognitive brilliance

Scintillations of somnambulant scents

Wafting down beaches

Bounded by

Oceans of mental madness

Infecting nostrils with

Harsh and pungent

Odors of epistemological

Understanding

I am the hourglass poet

Positioned between

Dimensions

Not yet realized

Morphing

Breath into health

Wealth into width

Height into posterity

Continuously

Flowing down

Wormholes

Granules

Of sand

Like time and space

Accumulate into

Parcels of style and grace

Making mountains

Piled high

Ruminating

Vertical visions

Illuminated

By horizontal

Reveries

I am the hourglass poet

Whose heart

Heaves heavy

Having lost

A Mighty Fine

Friend

Recently demised

Diminishing

The quality of life

Love

Functions like a pendulum

Counting

Polarities swings

Left to right

Back and Forth

Again

I grin

Through clinched teeth

With webbed feet

Sticking to the sides

Of this figure eight

Grasping realities

Structure

By the tail

My lungs swell

With pride

From having known him

I am the hourglass poet

Nursing wounds

Words

Wrapped in bandages

Of caring

Using gauzes of kindness

Medics gallantly

Attempt to save

My life

By

Transfusing

Tenses

Past

Present

Future

Like Four letter

Words

Light sabers

Concentrated

Into Beams

Being wielded

By spoken word warriors

Poets

Slamming nouns

Against verbs,

Like a Hadron Collider

Smashing

Pronouns

Against adjectives

Objecting

Strenuously

To mediocrity

I am the hourglass poet

Hosting tonight's

Open house

Where prescient prose

Meet

Prosaic poetry

Where the spotlight focuses

On a bar stool

Upon which sits

The hourglass of time

Constantly streaming

People's passion

Like Pebbles

Through life's timepiece

While above the stage

The neon sign reads

Welcome to

The hourglass café

564-5707 834-5183 Feb-8-1973 Thursday,

THE CULTURAL background of Blacks from the shores of Africa in the 1800's in their role in American history is portrayed by Bill Longmire and Renee Brown (above) in rehearsal Wednesday night of "Proud, Proud, Proud" to be presented Feb. 16 by the Chagrin Falls Park Community Center Youth Rap-In Committee and Diversity Station "Art Art" players. The events for Black History Week Series Feb. 12-19 include a film on Martin Luther King at Bainbridge town hall next Sunday and Monday.

VERENT MOMENT

Don Grauer and Sarah Morgan listen during Saturday's ceremonies for the Chagrin Valley Walk for Unity in Chagrin ...auer is with the Valley Presbyterian Church, in Chagrin Falls, ...organ is with the A.M.E Methodist Church in Bainbridge. More ...n page A6.

Month-Long Chagrin Falls Park Road Project Nears Completion

Reprinted from
THE CHAGRIN
VALLEY HERALD
Nov. 19, 1960

Convention proves pos

Anderson Hitchcock served as a volunteer at the Democratic Convention in Atlanta. (Aylsworth)

"We Shall Overcome" rings out in buccolic Chardon

BY BILL REEVES

VOLLEYBALL ACTION is a nightly pursuit of youths at the Chagrin Falls Park Community Center under the guidance of youth counselors such as William Vickers (in background).

AT HER DESK going over paper work is where Mrs. James Edwards is usually found. She is in charge of coordinating efforts to get the residents involved in the Community Action Program.

PLANNING A SKATING PARTY is just one of the many functions of youth workers such as Mrs. Elizabeth Lynch. Seen here discussing the good time to come are Debra Talley (left), Pamela Hitchcock, Mrs. Lynch, Norma and Valerie Crowley.

HOME CONSULTATIONS are part of the job of Miss Janet Greenhalf (left), family counselor under the Chagrin Falls Park Community Action Program. She's seen here discussing a problem with a mother of three preschoolers, Mrs. Al Walker of Rocker St. On the couch are Janice, 5, Jacqueline, 2, Mrs. Walker holding 3-month-old Paul, and Joyce, 5. Also participating in the conference is Mrs. N. S. Sharp, director of the preschool program.

ogram in High Gear

A PLACE OF OUR OWN:

The Chagrin Falls Park

from 1921 to 1950

by Andrew Wiese

for the Chagrin Falls Park Community Center

October, 1986

MELVIN STUBBS

AGE:	35
WEIGHT:	175
HEIGHT:	5'7"
HIGH SCHOOL:	KENSTON HIGH

NORMAN THOMPSON

AGE:	21
HEIGHT:	5'11"
WEIGHT:	240
HIGH SCHOOL:	LYNCH HIGH SCHOOL
COLLEGE:	UNIVERSITY OF KENTUCKY

DAVID TUCEK

AGE:	27
WEIGHT:	200
HEIGHT:	5'10"
HIGH SCHOOL:	KENSTON HIGH
COLLEGE:	HIRAM COLLEGE

PERSONALS —

JOHN BLOXSON....Self employed, Bloxson Hauling Service. He and wife Tina and son John, Jr. reside in Chagrin Falls Park.

ARTHUR BROOKS, JR. ....High School Basketball Varsity -- 2 years; 2nd team all conference East Cleveland Y.M.C.A. Most valuable player, Kenston Football, 1962. Most valuable player, Hiram College football, 1966. Director, Chagrin Falls Park Recreation Program, teaches at Kenston High School.

WILLIS T. BROWN .... Air Force All Stars. '56 Olympics, Melbourne, Australia. 3 times All Service, 2 times Air Force Scoring Champ. Semi-pro, 2 seasons Harlem's Hobo's; 3 seasons Harlem Ace's, Chicago; 5 seasons Mianord's All Stars, Weston, Va. Resides in Chagrin Falls Park with wife, Martha and two children.

JAMES BUCAR ....Coach; Chagrin Falls High School. Member, Olympic Sporting Good's Team. Quarterback, TruCast Touch Football Team, 1970. He and his wife Marianne are residents of Wickliffe, O.

DENNIS COBLE...Phys. Ed Director, Bessie Metzenbaum School. Service Co-ordinator, Ohio Athletic Association for Retarded. Vice Chairman, Ohio Jaycee's for Mental Health & Retardation, "Outstanding Young Educator's Award", Ohio, 1970. Lives in Bainbridge with wife Rene and son Christopher.

RONALD CONRAD ...He studied commercial art at Kent State. 2 years, U.S. Army. Salesman, Western and Southern Insurance Company.

JESSE DORSEY ... Chagrin Falls Park "Jets" . Advanced studies in neighborhood development and coordination of neighborhood resources, Case-Western Reserve.

BERNARD GRIFF ..."All County End" Football, 1956. 4 years, U.S. Navy. He is now in partnership with his father at Lowe's Greenhouse. He, and wife Laurine and children Jeff, Pam and Eric are residents of Bainbridge Ohio.

SAMUEL HALL ....He is employed at Mogul Chemical Company and is a member of Remias Smoother's Basketball team in Bainbridge Ohio.

FELTON HITCHCOCK .... Chagrin Falls Park "Jets". Employed at Chagrin Falls Park Community Center.

BOB KELLEN ....Teacher, Kenston High School. Bob's hobby is cave exploring. He was a member of the National Speleological Society. He and wife Martha and daughter Jennifer are residents of Chagrin Falls, Ohio.

JOHN PIAI ....Head Coach and History teacher, Chagrin Falls High School. Member, Olympic Sporting Goods Basketball Team. He, wife Cynthia and son Timothy are residents of Chagrin Falls, Ohio.

MELVIN STUBBS .... State Champ mile run, '54 and '55. State Champ 1/2 mile, '55. District Champ, '54 and '55. All county track mile run 3 years. Lives in Chagrin Falls Park with wife Jean and eight children. Employed by Eazor Express, Cleveland, Ohio.

NORMAN THOMPSON .... All C.V.C. title for three high school years. All state fullback, '67. Resides in Chagrin Falls Park with wife Linda and son Norman III. Employed at Kroger Warehouse, Solon, Ohio.

DAVID TUCEK ...Teacher and Assistant Coach, Kenston High School for three years. Hobby, motorcycle racing, won T-T Motorcycle race 1969-70. He and his wife Janyne live in Burton, Ohio. Employed with Allied Dealers Supply.

AN EDUCATIONAL SURVEY is part of the Community Action Program. Here, Art Brooks (left) gets the information he needs from Charles Sanders of Woodland Ave. Brooks, a former Park resident and Kenston High graduate, is now a Cleveland schoolteacher.

GRIN VALLEY HERALD   14 Pages   10 Cents

Park Community Center
Gets $24,000 Fund Grant

Gift of Cleveland Foundation will Pay Full-Time Director

C. of C. Calls Forum On District Problems

Kiwanis Show Opens Tonight

Citizens Group to Plug School Levy

Chagrin Park woman honored

CF Park Community Acti

BY ROY MEYERS

AN EXAMPLE OF FILTH is pointed out here by James C. Head Jr., who is working in the program as a housing specialist. Head is standing in the middle of a bed in a trash and garbage-filled house on S. Franklin Rd. Although the home is unoccupied, someone uses it nightly for a place to sleep. Head is working with county officials in an effort to have the house condemned.

Although the money still hasn't arrived from the Federal coffers in Washington, the Orange County Economic Opportunity Council is going full steam ahead with the Community By Action Program at Chapel Felix Park and it makes you wonder what they'd do if the dollars had the money.

James R. Jackson, director of the Park Community Center and co-ordinator of the Federal anti-poverty program for the CEOC, said he has been assured by the government that the money is forthcoming, but no one has told it up to far.

"In the meantime, the Federal officials told us to borrow the money to get things going," Jackson said.

THE COMMUNITY ACTION Program is being carried on in addition to the Operation Headstart program underway for pre-school youngsters at the Park Elementary School, both programs are being funded from a $20,771 grant approved earlier this year.

The Community Action Program (CAP) takes in the areas of housing, health, family economy, educational planning, small business, home management, neighborhood and neighborhood organizing.

"It's a broad program," said Jackson. "We're trying to get as many of the residents involved as we can. Many are being employed as paid staff and many others are helping voluntarily."

MRS. JAMES EDWARDS, who had been working as a secretary at the Community Center, has shifted over to the anti-poverty staff with the title of neighborhood specialist. She is responsible for contacting various segments of the neighborhood programs and reports directly to Jackson.

She's putting in at least 40 hours per week working with the Southern Council and other neighborhood groups and receiving $90 per month for her work.

"Mrs. Edwards' main task is to get the people involved," said Jackson. "She supervises the work of five youth workers who are assigned in getting the youngsters to participate in wholesome recreational activities.

"We're trying to show the kids

From left to right: Mr. Rodgers; Mr. Elijah Norman; Mr. Felton (Hunny) Hitchcock; Mr. Charles (Shug) Walker; Mr. Paris; Mr. Wheeler; Mr. Bloxsom; Mr. Hardy; Mr. Calvin Long; Mr. Huff; Mr. E.J. Lynch

(This photograph now hangs in the Black Firefighters Hall of Fame in Los Angeles, California)

CHAGRIN VALLEY ALL STARS

JOHN BLOXSON

AGE: 22
WEIGHT: 210
HEIGHT: 6'3"
HIGH SCHOOL: KENSTON

JESSE DORSEY

BIRTHDATE: 12-9-43
WEIGHT: 175
HEIGHT: 6'1"
HIGH SCHOOL: KENSTON
COLLEGE: C W B

ARTHUR BROOKS, JR.

BIRTHDATE: 6-3-43
WEIGHT: 180
HEIGHT: 5'10½"
HIGH SCHOOL: KENSTON HIGH
COLLEGE: HIRAM COLLEGE

BERNARD GRIFF

AGE: 33
WEIGHT: 215
HEIGHT: 6'4"
HIGH SCHOOL: KENSTON HIGH

WILLIS T. BROWN

BIRTHDATE: 8-10-38
WEIGHT: 185
HEIGHT: 6'0"
HIGH SCHOOL: TWINSBURG HIGH
COLLEGE: MARYLAND STATE

SAMUEL HALL

AGE: 18
WEIGHT: 145
HEIGHT: 5'6"
HIGH SCHOOL: KENSTON HIGH

JAMES BUCAR

AGE: 25
WEIGHT: 188
HEIGHT: 5'11"
HIGH SCHOOL: CHASE HIGH
COLLEGE: OHIO STATE

FELTON HITCHCOCK

BIRTHDATE: 4-8-49
HEIGHT: 185
HEIGHT: 6'0½"
HIGH SCHOOL: KENSTON HIGH

DENNIS COBLE

AGE: 21
WEIGHT: 165
HEIGHT: 5'6"
HIGH SCHOOL: LANCASTER CATH
COLLEGE: WEST VIRGINIA

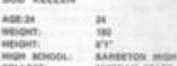

BOB KELLEN

AGE: 24
WEIGHT: 180
HEIGHT: 5'7"
HIGH SCHOOL: BARBERTON HIGH
COLLEGE: MURRAY STATE

RONALD CONRAD — Captain

AGE: 24
WEIGHT: 210
HEIGHT: 6'3"
HIGH SCHOOL: KENSTON HIGH
COLLEGE: KENT STATE

JOHN PIAI

AGE: 18
WEIGHT: 180
HEIGHT: 5'10"
HIGH SCHOOL: GREENSVILLE
COLLEGE: THIEL COLLEGE

RAISE A TOAST

Raise a toast to all my friends

The ones I love the most

Are my old friends

When the world

Starts closing in

I'll relax and then again

Raise a toast to all my friends

Raise a toast to all my friends

From coast to coast

They're my old friends

From Paris to New York

They will never sell me short

So I'll raise a toast

To all my friends

Raise a toast to all my friends

Raise a cheer to all not near

When it's the best that I can do

I'll raise a glass of wine or brew

And pose a toast to all my friends

Raise a toast to all my friends

Raise it up

With a great big grin

A hale and hearty one or two

That way

I'm not pie eyed

When I'm through

So, I'll raise a toast

To all my friends

Raise a toast to all my friends

I often brag and boast

About my old friends

The perfect time is Nye

For me

To raise my cell phone high

And place a call

To all my friends

WHEN GOD MET JUAN

When my friend's life

Came to an end

That's when his meeting

With God would begin

He mounted up

On angels wings

And flew toward heaven

As he began to sing

He soared up and away

Passed earth's atmosphere

Just for fun

He circled the Sun

At this orb

He left his terror

And his fear

As the solar winds

Dried up all of his tears

He made his way

Back

Past Mercury

And Mars

Depositing all of his

Anger among the stars

Like a comet

Streaking across the sky

Both Earth and Venus

Rocketed by

Saluting him

As in unison

Acknowledging that

His battle had been won

He passed

That behemoth Jupiter

Heading out into the galaxy

All greed was let go

Now

He knew he could relax

And enjoy the show

No more, envy

Hatred or rain

No more sunny days

Filled with pain

All is right now

With Juan my friend

As his meeting with god

Would soon begin

He hurtled outward

Through the cosmos

Waving to Neptune

Saturn and Uranus

On out into outer space

He sighed with relief

You could see it

In his face

When it dawned on him

That he had completed

Life's swift race

Pass Pluto

The center of the Milky Way

To the edges of the universe

15 billion light years away

He began to see

That celestial realm

Just then God

Took hold of the helm

Guided him right through

The pearly gates

Wait he exclaimed

Something is wrong here

As he surveyed

The gathered throng

This is not the heaven

Of Saint Peter or Saint Paul

But the heaven

Of Aztec warriors

Brave and tall

It was where

Juan had dreamed

Of being

After all

It was Quetzalcoatl

Who sat upon the throne

And his only word

To my friend Juan

Was "Bienvenido

Welcome Home"

VALERIE'S POEM

(It's in your eyes)

When rainbows crisscross

The skies

I can see it mirrored

Clearly in your eyes

X marks the spot

Where the pot

Of gold resides

And I can see it mirrored gently

In your eyes

It's in your eyes

Yes, it's in your eyes

It's in your eyes

Yes, it's in your eyes

Suns shimmering shown extra bright

Allowing me to see that sacred sight

Stars massage

Caress your face

Illuminating all of outer space

It was then and there

When I saw love's trace

Reflected through your smiling grace

It was then and there

When I realized

That I could see it mirrored

Clearly

In your eyes

It's in your eyes

Yes, it's in your eyes

It's in your eyes

Yes, it's in your eyes

From you

I first felt Love's tender touch

That I had always

Yearned and craved so much

Fragrant smells

Hung heavy in the air

Like precious jewels

Found seldomly rare

I watch

As your luminescent glow

Bathed you with a liquid halo

Suspended high above your head

Like a giant

Billowing cosmic pillow

Yet from the prism

Of your smiling heart

You let me know

Right from the very start

That the spot

Where the pot of gold resides

And all I ever really loved

Is mirrored in your eyes

It's in your eyes

Yes, it's in your eyes

It's in your eyes

Yes, it's in your eyes

A KWANZAA POEM

(The seven days of Kwanzaa)

On the first day of Kwanzaa

Ancestors gave to me

Umoja as Un-i-ty

On the second day of Kwanzaa

Swahili helped me see

Kugichagulia

Self Determination

And Umoja as Un-i-ty

On the third day of Kwanzaa

Karenga gave to me

Collective Work Ujima

Kugichagulia

Self Determination

And Umoja as Un-i-ty

On the fourth day of Kwanzaa

Ujamma is the word

Collective Economics

Collective work Ujima

Kugichagulia

Self Determination

And Umoja as Un-i-ty

On the fifth day of kwanzaa

Libations do we pour

Nia that's our purpose

Cooperative Economics

Collective Work Ujima

Kugichagulia

Self Determination

And Umoja as Un-i-ty

On the sixth day of Kwanzaa

Kuumba sets us free

With Crea-tiv-i-ty

Nia that's our purpose

Cooperative Economics

Collective work Ujima

Kugichagulia

Self Determination

And Umoja as Unity

On the Seventh Day of Kwanzaa

Imani rules the day

Faith is what's required

Kuumba sets us free

With Cre-a-tiv-i-ty

Nia that's our purpose

Cooperative Economics

Collective work Ujima

Kugichagulia

Self Determination

And Umoja as Un-i-ty

The Wind Chime Tree

A Short Play

By

© Anderson Hitchcock

3502 W. Slauson Ave.

Los Angeles, Ca 90043

Tel: 323-898-3064

trinitycrossfoundation@yahoo.com

Characters:

Genie—Grandmother (deceased)

Lula Mae—Mother (early thirties)

Ghenea—Granddaughter (about twelve)

Places:

Graveyard scene—Rest land Cemetery. Mother and daughter standing over grandmother's grave, beneath tree filled with wind chimes.

Grandmother is on the Front Porch of family home, as an apparition sitting in a rocking chair. Doesn't speak, but is a constant presence.

Flute begins to play amazing grace while lights are still down. As lights come up flute fades and Mother and daughter stand in graveyard next to grave of Grandmother (Genie) with tree in the background. Lula Mae begins to speak to her daughter (Ghenea).

Mother (Lula Mae)

Your grandmother was a very strong woman Ghenea and I wanted to make sure that you knew how great of a woman she was. She was a black woman ahead of her time in many ways. I remember many days we would sit on the front porch and she would tell me about the breast cancer that finally killed her. She was always in pain there toward the end. However, in spite of the pain, she would always say, "Life is Good and God is Better".

Daughter (Ghenea)

Is that what Grandma died of Breast Cancer?

Mother (Lula Mae)

That's exactly what killed her. She had both of her breasts in what they call a radical mastectomy. Think that you are old enough to know the truth and to understand why I go annually for the doctor or nurse to examine my breasts in addition to scheduling my annual mammogram. Before long, you will begin to grow breasts, have your first period, which we have discussed before, and become a young woman. It's best that I begin to educate you now that learning and practicing monthly breast self exam is an important step that you can take to protect your health.

Daughter (Ghenea)

Why do they call it a radical mastectomy Mommy?

Mother (Lula Mae)

They call it a radical mastectomy, because some women go as far as having both of their breasts completely removed in the hopes that they will become cancer free and live longer and healthier lives. Other women chose to remove only the affected breast, yet if found early only a lumpectomy, removing the tumor needs to be done. Early detection and education is essential. Your grandmother was a remarkable woman. One year after her lumpectomy, chemotherapy and radiation.

She dedicated her life to educate the community and help other women. She started the organization that I now head, "Love Your Breasts Incorporated" to help other black women with the disease to know that inner strength and outer beauty can co-exist in the aftermath of breast cancer.

Ghenea

That's a funny name for an organization. Do men have an organization called "love your penis incorporated"?

Lula Mae

Yeah, they do. It's called the National Football League. That's why your father spends so much time in front of the TV on weekends. Men do get breast cancer but it is primarily a women's disease, and that is why women must take responsibility for finding the cure. That is the reason that your grandmother made me promises to keep the organization going. She also left some money to send you to college to become a doctor, so you can help find a cure.

Ghenea

What causes breasts cancer Mommy?

Lula Mae

That's what they are trying to find out baby. They have many different opinions, such as; that antiperspirants, might clog up the pores under the arms, too much fat and sugar in our diet, but as of now we need more research to determine what the causes are and how to protect ourselves from getting breast cancer.

Ghenea

So is that why you insist upon me studying biology, chemistry, and all those science classes that I don't like?

Lula Mae

That's right Darling, I need you to be prepared to take over this organization and keep the fight going to find a cure for this terrible disease.

Ghenea

Okay Mommy, you can count on me. I will study hard and be prepared when I graduate from Medical school to contribute to the research on curing breast cancer.

At this point, the wind chimes in the tree begin to clang and begin to make a considerable noise, which interrupts the conversation.

Ghenea

Why are all those wind chimes in that tree Mama?

Lula Mae

Your grandmother loved wind chimes. She collected all of those wind chimes over the years. We use to sit on her porch and listen to the wind blow through the wind chimes. It made such a beautiful sound. So when she died I placed her favorite wind chime in a tree near her grave. Your grandmother would always say "Whenever wind chimes chime a woman has been diagnosed free of breast cancer."

(Fade to Genie sitting on the front porch in a chair talking to Lula May. Lula Mae is not in the scene, but it is clear that the conversation is directed towards her. It is obvious that the disease is having an effect on her health and she is talking with some difficulty.)

Genie

Lula Mae, I want you to make sure that you keep Love Your Breast, Inc. going, okay? You know that black women suffer disproportionately with breast cancer, yet the major breast cancer organizations don't pay much attention to women of color. That is why I started Love Your Breasts, Inc. The women in the community thought that I was crazy, but over the years we have worked with hundreds of Women, who are now survivors of breast cancer. It hasn't been easy but we have managed. Now it is up to you to keep it going and disperse information and hope to women of color who are suffering from this terrible disease.

When I make my transition I want you to place one of these wind chimes at my grave as a symbol of the fight against breast cancer and begin to offer them for sale to other families that have gone through a similar struggle, use it as a way to raise money and consciousness about the disease. I will always be with you Lula Mae; I love you and think the world of you.

Lula Mae

I love you mom and think the world of you too!

Fade into black and light comes up back on Lula Mae and Ghenea at the graveyard. Wind chimes still clanging

Ghenea

Now I understand Mommy. Grandma was a very heroic women and I will carry on the tradition that you both started. You mean to tell me that all of these wind chimes represent women that have passed from breast cancer.

Lula Mae

That is exactly right Ghenea. When your grandmother died, I placed the first wind chime in that tree over there. I saw it as a way of always having your grandmother with me, no matter where I went. The first thing that I would do is hang a wind chime outside of my door and when the wind blew and the wind chime would clang, I always thought about my mother. It always comforted me, and I could still hear her voice talking to me and telling me to be strong and to carry on.

So over the years, we have sold thousands of wind chimes and the money has gone to continue the work that your grandmother started of giving support, comfort, hope and information to women of color suffering with this daunting disease.

Not only do we provide transportation to and from doctors' appointments, but also we go with them for the surgery and once they recover enough, we provide whatever support they need, whether it is emotional counseling, wigs, make up, prosthetics, or whatever. We even go in and wash dishes, or help with housework, if they need it. We also have a support group for women that meets every month in neighborhoods all around the State.

We also have a bi-monthly" Look Good, Feel Better Program" because women are always concerned about their looks. This program is great for women experiencing the negative side effects of cancer treatment.

Ghenea

Wow Mommy, you and grandma are my heroes. I want to be just like the two of you, when I grow up, helping women to help themselves overcome all obstacles and finally beat this disease, so we don't have to plant more trees and hang more wind chimes.

Lula Mae

Well, I hope we will always have wind chime trees to remind us of our sisters, mothers and daughters who were taken from us at a much too early age, but are still talking to us through the Wind Chime Trees and are the real heroes. People can order their wind chimes, or make a contribution to Love Your Breasts, Inc., at www.lybi.org, again that Web Site is www.lybi.org.

I love you Ghenea and think the world of you.

Ghenea

I love you too mommy and think the world of you and always remember, "Life is Good and God is Better"

Mother and daughter smile at each other and as they embrace, the lights fade to black, while flute begins to play softly the song, Hero by Enrique Iglesias

ABOUT THE AUTHOR

The author, Anderson Hitchcock is an accomplished musician. A flute player trained at the Conservatory of Music at the University of Alaska in Fairbanks, who subsequently studied flute at Cuyahoga City College in Cleveland, Ohio and at the Conservatory of Music at San Jose City College. He plays Gospel, Classical and Jazz music and now resides in Los Angeles, California. The author has two children, Ghenea who is in the tenth grade, and Mori, who just graduated from the Science and Discover High school in Chester, Pennsylvania, where they live with their mother, Clara. Anderson met Clara in Jamaica in 1991, while on vacation. They soon married and Clara moved to the USA in 1992 and in August of 1993 they had their first Child Mori, and then four years later they had Ghenea. Mori will be attending Juniata College, in Northeastern Pennsylvania.

Anderson has an Associate Degree from Foothill College, where he received a scholarship to study at Santa Clara University and matriculated in 1975. From Santa Clara Anderson went to Case Western Reserve University, where he studied Law at George Gund School of Law, and ended up completing his course work there for a Master Degree in Non Profit Management from the Mandel Center for Non Profit Administration in 1992.

Anderson has black belts in *Soo Bahk Do-Moo Duk Kwan,* and has also studied *Haidong Gumdo* a Korean sword and staff discipline. Anderson has traveled extensively in Africa, Asia and Europe, as a gemologist and diamond miner. He has lived in Angola and Namibia West Africa for a number of years pursuing his passion for gem quality stones. He has studied martial arts in Seoul, Korea, and in 1995 participated in the 50-year anniversary of Soo Bahk Do-Moo Duk Kwan in Korea, with his Grand Master, Hwang Kee and over five thousand other black belts from throughout the world. He has worked with martial arts, mathematics and music for three decades and continues to do so, every Friday as a volunteer at Zion Hill Baptist Church in Los Angeles. Yes, that's right, Zion Hill Baptist, a church of the same name and as it turns out, and the same origins as the church on the cover of the book.

Coincidently both Churches as it turns are were founded by members who had relocated from the same Church in Cleveland, Ohio in the 1920's and that Church as it turns out, was New Hope Baptist. Research is now under way to see if the link between the two Churches can be found. It proves, Contrary to one great American writer, that you can go home again.

This is the second book by the author. In 2009, Anderson published through (i universe) "Economics as a Second Language" creating wealth one family reunion at a time. Focus of the book, is the building and operation of Black Family Reunion Resorts at which economics as a second language will be taught and the spending power of the community around family reunions galvanized into a force to create, jobs, wealth and assets for one of the consistently poorest segments of society in the United States of America. Purchase "Economics as a Second Language on line by going to www.trinitycrossfoundation.org, the Trinity Cross Website and buy it, while contributing to the work of the Trinity Cross Foundation. Thank you in advance for your support.

<u>Wishing you and your family Health, Wealth and Prosperity.</u>

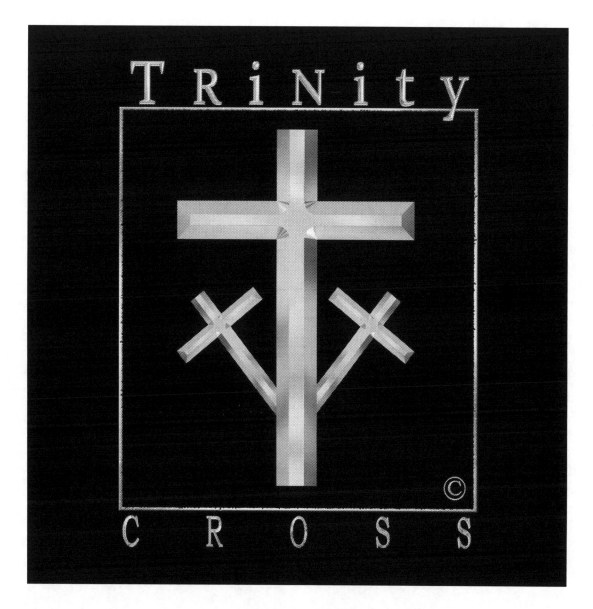

TRINITY CROSS©

A SYMBOL OF HEALTH—WEALTH—PROSPERITY

This Trinity Cross-was given to me in a dream while I was visiting some friends in the Bronx, New York in 2007 while I was on my way to Africa. Over the years, I have traveled to after via JFK in New York and always enjoy my visits with the Darling Family, with whom I have been friends for a number of years.

The voice in the dream explained, "I am going to give you an updated version of the cross after over 2000".

I immediately said in response to the speaker, whom I assumed to be GOD "Why me" to which the voice promptly responded "Why not you". The voice went on to say that, I am giving you a new dispensation of HEALTH, WEALTH AND PROSPERITY, after 2000 years, which this cross represents. According to the voice, whoever displays this symbol, either on their person, in their home, or in their car, or anywhere of significance to them, is destined for HEALTH WEALTH AND PROSPERITY.

The Trinity Cross-has now become the symbol for the Trinity Cross Foundation, non-profit, non-governmental organization, whose purpose for being is to aide famine victims throughout the African Diaspora. The initial focus of our work has been focused primarily with Somalia and the Horn of Africa.

Working closely with Dr. Osman Mohamed, originally from Mogadishu, Somalia we have adapted a concrete plane for intervention and assistance, but we need your help. We have begun the process of aiding those throughout the world who are members of the African Diaspora. African Americans form a vital link to great wealth and resources here in the United States that can assist to aide those who are dying from starvation and being slaughtered as collateral damage in endless civil wars.

The Trinity Cross Foundation is dedicated to raising awareness of and money for relief aide to be purchase and airlifted to those that are in desperate need of our help. African Americans have for so long been absent from the world scene as major players in situations of starvation and deprivation. The Trinity Cross Foundation seeks to turn that inactivity into an avalanche of caring.

PLEASE WON'T YOU HELP US TO HELP THEM? Contribute today. All contributions are tax exempt and tax deductible. Go to www.trinitycrossfoundation.org and make your contribution to the future of those less fortunate.

If you would like to help the Trinity Cross Foundation with its work, please go to our website trinitycrossfoundation.org and buy a cross or two, or a set, or make a tax free contribution. You can also send a check to Trinity Cross Foundation, 3502 W. Slauson Ave, suite 296, Los Angeles, California 90043. You may also contact us by email at trinitycrossfoundation@yahoo.com, or follow us on tweeter @andersonhitchcock, or call me at 323-898-3064.

DONATE YOUR UNUSED OR OLD VEHICLE TODAY!

RECEIVE A TAX DEDUCTION

CALL 855-500-7433

Anderson Hitchcock

TELL IT LIKE IT TIS, NOT LIKE IT TWAS (JT'S POEM)

Overalls languish limply

On his emaciated frame

Pockets filled with rejection

And little else

Face weathered

Mirror

Frozen time

Reflecting

Wine soaked

Diatribes of delusion

Thunder Bird

Fueled dreams

Regurgitated in rhyme

Tell it like it tis

Not like it twas

This refrain

Echoing

Reminders

Of long forgotten

Hopes and schemes

Darting

Like comets

In and out

Of consciousness

Sparkling

Glimmering

All too briefly

Then burning out

Like shooting stars

Upon re-entry into

Realities realm

JT struts among

Fallow fields

To find

The embalmed corpses

Of his youth

Serenely embedded

Between wrinkles

Severely wrought

From Life's lessons

Not learned

Hard knocks not heeded

Head still unbowed

From multiple shocks

Administered over time

A human absorber

That neither cushions

The blows

Nor soothes the pain

Tell it like it Tis

Not like it twas

Acts as a salve

A Savior savant

Of the silent

The Unheard

The invisible hero

Of disabused Debutantes

Dallying over

Daily doses of dementia

Mixed with liberal amounts

Of distilled spirits

Which constantly invoke

Delicious dalliances

Of a perpetual rebirth

Of his childhood

Tell it like it tis

Not like it twas

Faint shadows of a man

Protrude from work boots

Worn more for fashion

Than functionality

Not pay check earned

But labor scorned

A clarion call

To the elements

Goes out

Incomprehensible too many

To most

Conversations with daffodils

In languages

Loss of succor

Medieval chants

Concocted in dungeons

Where speech is prescribed

Not by its beauty

But by tongues

Pierced through

With stakes

While jaws wired shut

Circumscribe the screams

Of those

Being cremated

While yet still alive

Tell it like it tis

Not like it twas

Inebriation

Becomes

His muse

His mating call

Mimics

The cry of a hawk

Who sits on his?

Master's arm

With talons

Well sharpened

Ready for the hunt

His prey

However

Disappears

Against the backdrop

Of stationary skies

AUTHOR'S STATEMENT

I have wanted to write this book, all of my life. Some of my earliest recollections about growing up in Chagrin Falls Park, or the Park, as its residents, past and future referred to it, compelled me to tell this story, this story about growing up in this Northeastern Ohio community, were I remember having the feeling of being a part of some grand experiment, not just the common experience for Black people during this period, not just the awareness of racism, or of social, and political stagnation, or of the malaise, which led us once per month, during the winter months to Chardon, the County Seat, to pick-up commodities of powdered milk, spam and other canned goods, in order to survive persistent bouts of, no work for my father, when because of the weather and the fact that he was the only black man working for Miller Plumbing and Heating Company in Chagrin Falls, and was therefore consistently the first to be laid off, and sometimes the only person without a job during the winter. More importantly, however, I remember a sense that my parents, along with the entire community served as a backdrop for the Black version of a Norman Rockwell America.

An America, in which, through hard work and perseverance, everything is supposed to be possible, and while excuses can abound, it became clear to me that the will of the human spirit is indeed stronger than any perceived inferiority, based upon the color of one's skin, or the shape of one's skull. I value the life; I lived growing up and would not have traded it for the world.

An experiment, in which a bold group of pioneers had set out, in a virtual wilderness, to build their American dream and satisfy the eternal quest for a place of their own in the sun has proven the strength of the human spirit, against all odds and obstacles. A fulfillment of the closely held scripture, that "Through God all things are possible".

This book is dedicated to the brave men and women who settled in Chagrin Falls Park, conquered their fears and inhibitions, and fought bravely to raise families and live their lives on their own terms, as free men and women.

I was born in St. Luke's hospital in Cleveland, Ohio on August 25th of 1947 the same hospital where my son Mori would be born in 1993, 46 years later. Ghenea, my daughter was born nearly four years later at Cleveland Clinic. I have maintained a lifelong connection with Chagrin Falls Park, Ohio. A relationship, that allows me to be both proud, and ashamed, concurrently.

Proud of the courage and conviction of the residents of the community and ashamed by treatment of this community and its residents by the powers that be in the City of Chagrin Falls, The Township of Bainbridge and the County of Geauga, possibly with the either the active or passive collusion of the State of Ohio.

My parents, Felton and Lula Hitchcock, already had two children, Felton and George in back to back years and I represented the third child in 3 years. In three years 1945, 1946 and 1947, my mother bore three sons. I, along with my two brothers was educated at Chagrin Falls Park Elementary School, which was located in the center of the community and was a one room, seven grade school house. In this one room school house the people of Chagrin Falls Park realized the dream of educating their Chagrin free of the racial animus as prevalent in society as a whole. They succeeded admirably and should be remembered as the trailblazers that they clearly were.

The teachers hired, that had such a huge impact on my life and the lives of everyone who came through that school taught everything from social studies to math. They traveled daily from Cleveland, which is about an hour drives away, and, in my humble opinion provided an afro-centric education, second to none.

Their focus was on providing a quality education for their students, and equally as importantly, they made sure to provide a solid understanding of the accomplishments of African Americans throughout history, and had us dream that we could and would do things of equal value. From Sojourner Truth to Toussaint Le Overture, the history of the African Diaspora was central to the lessons taught in this elementary school.

The teachers were Mr. Aiken and Mr. Clark, who were the Principals, the first grade teacher was Mrs. Gay, second grade teacher was Mrs. Chambers, and the third grade teacher was Mrs. Reed. Mrs. Wilkerson and Ms. Connors who taught fourth and fifth grades, respectively. I also remember Mr. Clark was the principal and Mr. Snyder was a fifth grade teacher.

This book, in sum, represents their determined efforts to provide the means for a quality education. I would like to use this book to salute them all for a job well done.

AUTHOR'S HISTORY

I graduated from the first grade as an honor student, along with my cousin Robert Watson as the Valedictorian in an elaborate cap and gown graduation ceremony, which was held at Zion Hill Missionary Baptist Church in Chagrin Falls Park.

This first inclination of academic prowess presaged a lifetime of educational involvement, which lead eventually to study at 11 Colleges and Universities In 1960 I graduated from the seventh grade and for the first time was thrust into the larger world outside of Chagrin Falls Park as an eighth grader at Kenston High School. For the first time I was exposed to racial antagonism and prejudice at this predominantly white school, but that is a story for a different time.

Chagrin Falls Park Elementary school was a community school in every sense of the word. At noon, the children were dismissed and walked home for lunch and at 1:30 pm. walked back to school for the second half of the day. There was also a playground that the parents built for the children, which had a merry go round, sliding board, teeter tauter, a basketball court and a gravel area for running and playing tag. It was indeed a wonderful way for the children to learn and to interact with one another.

Every summer, the school would put on a play in the parking area of the school and the parents would build a stage upon which the play would be performed. I remember one summer in particular, in which the production was Seventy Six Trombones. I remember marching across the stage as if in a marching band and singing along with the music.

The entire community turned out for the production and it was a tremendous success in that all of the children got to perform in front of their parents and the community as a whole. The teachers were committed to their jobs, to the community, to the children collectively, and each child, individually and helped me to form my opinions about the nature of commitment, both to myself and to the wider world which lay beyond the community. This was during the polio epidemic and I remember vividly the day that the nurses and doctors came to give inoculations to all of the children. This was a day of celebration and of concern jointly, so the parents came to be with the children as they received the shots.

Some of the parents had a hard time controlling their children who were afraid of the needles. I don't think that we had ever seen so many white people in our community and there was a sense of foreboding, but things went well and everyone received their inoculations with only minor inconveniences.

I only relate these stories as a way of bringing you into the world that motivated me in my initial learning experiences and set the tone for much of what has transpired in the proceeding fifty five years and allowed for the development of these poems and reveries. I cannot imagine growing up in a better environment for a child, who exemplified the classic wide-eyed approach to a sometimes daunting, yet always wonder filled world.

These poems and reveries have been floating around in my consciousness forever and a day and I feel fortunate finally to be able to put them down in this book. *Have you heard the sidewalk cricket sing* was one of the earliest poems that I wrote, and seeks to explore the difference between crickets that I grew up listening to out in the country, and ones that I heard while living in cities from New York, New York to Los Angeles, California.

While living in cities as diverse as Luanda, Angola and Fairbanks, Alaska, I was always observant of nature and perceived my life experiences as intimately connected with my surroundings. I am sure the differences are minimal but for my sensibilities, the differences were monumental.

I would like to thank my siblings for the lessons that they taught me about life, which includes but are limited to love, caring, kindness, toughness and companionship. As one of six children, one of the things I appreciate the most about my brothers and sisters is that I never felt alone and never felt the sting of loneliness.

They were always there and always looking out for me and after me. I want to say a sincere thank you to, each and every one of them. Milton, the brother just under me is no longer with us, he made his transition in 2008 in Denver, Colorado and I would like to thank his wife, Sharon for being so kind and loving. To other brothers, Felton, George, and William, and to my sister Florine, I want to say I love you and think the world of each of you. Thank you for being my siblings.

I also want to acknowledge, my relatives, my grandparents, Genie and Luke Walker and my grandparents on the Hitchcock side and all my uncles and aunts on the Hitchcock side, my uncles; James and Shug Walker and uncle Milton, my aunties; Ella, Alma, Virginia, Matt, Margie and Dee Dee, as well as my cousins; Larry; Clinton; Grady; Marlena; Bobby; Alvin; Charlie; Mickey; Marilyn; Charmaine; Everett; Nicky; Velma; Candy; Gloria; Frieda; Fred; Jerome; Sherri; and George. The Long; Denson; and Watson, and Beck family were related through marriage. In addition, I would like to ask those that I neglected to name, to please forgive me in this moment of dementia.

Of special merit, I would like to highlight my childhood friends. Fortunately, for me there were many, but those most special to my development, would have to be Phil Simmons, Tim Dorsey, and Bob, Willie and Clarence (wine) Harris, now both deceased.

The Harris' became my home away from home, and I spent many a day and night, with Poor Joe and Julia, who were like my second set of parents. While growing up in the Park had its own special qualities, it also had its dangers.

I choose not to go, extensively, into them in this book, perhaps in another book in the future. Suffice it to say, that there was no guarantee that one would survive the rough and tumble nature of the Park, and many succumbed to turf wars, bullets, stabbings, drunken brawls and the general mayhem of a community struggling to survive and eke out its place in a sometimes hostile world.

While my father's family did not live in Chagrin Falls Park, but in Cleveland; therefore my interactions with them were extremely limited. We rarely left the Park, and for someone to drive out for a visit, was more than just a notion, but had all of the ear markings of a road trip. I do want to acknowledge them as well.

My Grandfather and Grandmother, Anderson and Anna Hitchcock, along with their children Milton, Jimmie, Edrick and Aunt Sue formed my father's side of my genetic makeup, and I am grateful to them for providing some good genetic material.

I also have too many people to name, that are as responsible for inspiring me to write this book, as are my relatives, and who have been intimately involved in shaping my thoughts on the content and makeup of this book. I thank them dearly. I also want particularly, to thank Daniel Berry, of the Cleveland Growth Association.

Who during my time at the Mandel Center for Non Profit Management, became my mentor and my friend, and exposed me to the high finance world that allowed for the building of the Science and Technology Museum, the Rock and Roll Hall of Fame and the new Cleveland Browns Stadium.

He subsequently hired me as an Intern with the Foundation in the area of Economic Development. I will always be grateful for his support of me and the Family Reunion Concept that came out of my work there.

This was during a period in which I was attempting to rally the residents of Chagrin Falls Park in order to purchase Harris's farm, a 100-acre parcel directly adjacent to Chagrin Falls Park, separately Chagrin Falls from its poorer neighbor to the north Chagrin Falls Park.

Daniel Berry lead a panel of local officials from Chagrin Falls, Bainbridge County and Bentleyville, to discuss the potential for building a family reunion resort on that property that could provide and economic injection of jobs and a measure of hope for a better future to those living in the Park.

Because the railroad track that ran between Solon, through Bentleyville, and through Chagrin Falls Park to the center of Chagrin Falls proper, it was envisioned that there could be a tram built to connect both villages with a winery and family reunion that could be built on the horse farm adjacent to the Park. The ride would be natural breathtaking and scenic and would have been unique for the flora and fauna of this area. The area now has, Sea World Park, and Geauga Lake, and would have been a mere stone's throw from the proposed Family Reunion Resort/Winery.

Chagrin Falls Winery would have been a huge success, and increase tourism in the area considerably. For his willingness to support such an idea while those in the community thought it useless, meant the world to me and gave the confidence needed to pursue this and other extreme remedies to impoverishment and hopelessness for the population of Chagrin Falls Park.

I must call attention to my Father, Felton Hitchcock Senior, who was known as a jack-of-all-trades in the Park and could fix everything from furnaces to electric fixtures. He worked moist of his life as a plumber for Miller Plumbing and Heating in Chagrin Falls proper and was one of the few black men that were able to secure employment outside of at the paper mill, which was left over from earlier days.

My father, I recall was a very able man, with numerous skills at his disposal. He could be counted on if your car broke down, if your plumbing sprung a leak, if you needed a new roof. There seemed to be nothing, my father could not repair, and while he liked to work alone, on some occasions he would allow me to assist him.

when assisting was out of the question, either because, I was too young, the work was too dangerous, or he was just in one of his moods, which he seemed to be in quite a bit, he would allow me sometimes to watch, as he poured the concrete for the basement, to one of the three houses we lived in while we were growing up, fixing the roof, repairing the car, or just working around the house, it was always a pleasure to observe him in his element.

My Father seemed to be happiest when he was working. He had quite a temper, which he would vent on me and my other sibling, on a regular basis, but he was a good provider.

I remember as a child, my father who had built somewhat of a temporary home, that was none too sturdy, decided to build a better structure. The problem was that at the time, there were three children and there was no place for us to move while the new home was under construction. The solution that my father came up with was to build the new house around the old one. In a stroke of pure genius, I will never forget living in this one room cabin, while my father and men from the communities worked tirelessly to construct our new home.

After a few months, the best I can remember, the new home was complete, and my father and the others tore down the one room house and threw it out of the window of the new home. Without missing a beat, my father had done the incredible and we were in our new home. The importance of the new home is that it had an indoor bathroom, a furnace instead of a cold stove and running water.

I was seven or eight at the time, but I will never forget how proud I was of my father and still how proud of him I am today. Whenever I return to Chagrin Falls Park today, I still have people come up to me and tell me what a great man my father was in their eyes. Needless to say, it does wonders for my little ego.

I can honestly say that my father and I had a tenuous relationship as father and son. While I loved him, he was a very difficult man to love, even though he was my father and I must say that as I got older and he and my mother divorced, to me as a teen it was one of the happiest periods of my life.

I would be truly remiss if I did not mention the community center, which truly served as a center for the community and brought all of the various factions of the community. The Park was a conglomeration of six Churches, five bars, several local stores, which sold the basic products, a gas station, several garages and ice cream parlor, barber shops and plenty of colorful characters and personalities in the Park, The community center acted to bring them all together; sometimes successfully and others times not. Altogether, it played the leading role as a voice for the community.

While, Bruce Constance was hired as the first Executive Director of a newly constructed community center structure, and also the first director that had been born and raised in the Park, he proved to be equally as useless as those that had immediately preceded him.

All other Directors had been from outside of the community, and had directed activities in the former mink ranch, which had limited utility, but served its purpose proudly. In my opinion, the directors, one and all, enriched themselves at the expense of the community; but those are stories for another book.

Ms. Preston and Mr. Waters were the two directors who in my opinion understood the historic nature of the community and sought constantly to support the inherent strengths within the community, while the others seemed more like conspirators, who had been planted in the community to subvert, divert and in some way personally benefit from the community. Carpetbaggers would have been a kind description of the roles that they played in the drama that is Chagrin Falls Park and its community center.

While I had been part of the interview process for the directorship of the Center in the late nineties, I felt throughout the process that the fix was in to hire Bruce Constance and James Jackson and Martha Dorsey working in collusion had decided it in advance.

My qualifications, having completed my course work at Case Western Reserve University, Mandel Center for Non Profit Management, a few years earlier qualified me to be the first director of the Center, ever to have been born, raised and educated in the community and to now lead the community through the Community Center, would have been momentous, but It was not to be, however and Bruce Constance was hired as the new Executive Director.

I certainly would claim that there was malfeasance on the part of the Board of Directors for hiring him. He was woefully under-qualified for the job. But his hiring allowed both Martha and Jackson to manipulate him in his position. This episode was the excuse that the forces in Bainbridge Township needed to take control o f the community center and thereby the community as a whole. In my opinion sealed the fate of the community and two people must bear responsibility for this outrageous situation developing.

At the time he was hired for the directorship of the Community Center, Bruce was the manager/owner of a janitorial service, and would have been perfect as contractor for janitorial services for the new facility, but was imminently under qualified as an Executive Director.

Perhaps the Board of Directors of the Center, including Martha Dorsey and James Jackson wanted to kill two birds with one stone, which fiscally would have been a smart move, but I do not believe that was their objective.

I do not make these allegations spuriously, or without considerable thought. I believe that the Board of Directors, and especially James Jackson, who in my opinion, had long since outlived his usefulness to the community, if he had ever had any, along with Martha Dorsey conspired with others to hire Bruce , who subsequently had to resign the position, or face Charges of corruption and conspiracy to commit fraud.

While some of what I write in this book comes from anecdotal information and lacks empirical facts, I believe that the supposition, in my mind certainly warrants further investigation by those representatives of the law in these matters.

Though most of the history of this community is wrapped in mystery and surrounded by a wall of denial, I believe the truth is definitely out there for those interested in discovering it.

I would love an investigation by the Ohio State's Attorney General's Office to determine the validity or lack thereof of the charges that I have made against the cabal, led by Mr. Jackson who ran, and could in some way still be running the community center to their benefit and to the detriment of the residents of Chagrin Falls Park.

The community center was a converted mink ranch, and while the mink has a certain special quality, there is no doubt that those of us who grew up in the Park have and equality special character. I would like to express my sincere thanks and appreciation to them for providing much of the inspiration I used to compile book.

In this book I have included photos of my parents Lula and Felton Hitchcock, other members of my family and a few photos that assist in telling the story of this tiny community tucked away in Northeastern Ohio, in the heart of it All. I grew quite fond of saying that "If Ohio is the heart of it all, and then the patient must be comatose"

I would like to take this opportunity to thank those that contributed photos to this effort. I would like to thank my cousin Tyrone Beck, Ralph Jones and Demeteres Johnson, at the community center. I also want to thank Rose and Roland Motley, Pat Sanders and Harriet Bolden for their efforts, which were without success. I spoke with a number of people in Chagrin Falls in an attempt to get as much photo documentation as I could, and what you see is what emerged from those attempts.

I hope you enjoy this sometimes-tortuous walk down memory lane as I did compiling this book. The thoughts, stories and opinions expressed in this book are all mine. I cannot say that I have tried to be fair and balanced in my treatment of issues and individuals raised in this telling of the story, but to where possible I have attempted to be accurate, within the license taken by any teller of stories. Please take them with a grain of salt and remember, "Too much salt causes high blood Pressure". Here's wishing you and me continued grace under life's pressures.

Future editions are planned so please send additional photos to Anderson Hitchcock at 3502 W. Slauson Avenue, Los Angeles, California 90043, or email them to crenshawmerchants1@ yahoo.com